The Justice Women

The Justice Women

The Female Presence in the Criminal Justice System 1800-1970

Stephen Wade

First published in Great Britain in 2015 by
Pen & Sword History
an imprint of
Pen & Sword Books Ltd
47 Church Street
Barnsley
South Yorkshire
S70 2AS

ISBN 978 1 47384 365 3

A CIP catalogue record for this book is available from the British Library

Typeset in Ehrhardt by
Mac Style Ltd, Bridlington, East Yorkshire
Printed and bound in the UK by CPI Group (UK) Ltd,
Croydon, CRO 4YY

Pen & Sword Books Ltd incorporates the imprints of Pen & Sword Archaeology, Atlas, Aviation, Battleground, Discovery, Family History, History, Maritime, Military, Naval, Politics, Railways, Select, Transport, True Crime, and Fiction, Frontline Books, Leo Cooper, Praetorian Press, Seaforth Publishing and Wharncliffe.

For a complete list of Pen & Sword titles please contact
PEN & SWORD BOOKS LIMITED
47 Church Street, Barnsley, South Yorkshire, S70 2AS, England
E-mail: enquiries@pen-and-sword.co.uk
Website: www.pen-and-sword.co.uk

Contents

Preface

As in most professions, the experience of women working in the justice system is that of belonging to a minority and operating in a culture determined by male needs and behaviours. Women in the justice professions have an experience that is more heightened. Crime is an overwhelmingly male generated problem. As I write these words, men make up 95 per cent of the prison population of England and Wales. And so many of the tiny minority of women in prison have had their lives blighted by male abuse. All the more important then, that women should play a greater role in finding the solutions to crime and anti-social behaviour in our communities and reduce the re-offending rates of those who pass through the justice system.

The position of women in operational criminal justice roles remains a fascination. Despite recent increases in the numbers of women in senior operational roles, many people express surprise that women choose to work in professions that are dominated by male managers and are focused on controlling male offenders.

I started my career twenty-seven years ago as a probation officer and have been a prison governor for the past twenty years. Over this time I have seen many changes. Although many of the issues faced by women in the criminal justice system are now different and opportunities have increased, we still have to work hard to be seen as equal and also to challenge male assumptions.

I hope this book will offer insight into an exciting and socially significant career path. Just over a century ago the law disqualified women from working in the field. So there has been a transformation. But women still face challenges in achieving advancement and in influencing the operational agenda. Above all, I hope that young women today will be inspired by the experiences of those who have gone before and feel able to participate in this rewarding field of work.

Lynn Saunders
Governor
HM Prison Whatton

Introduction

A photograph of Betty Lindley taken at the Bassano Studio in 1914 signifies a revolution in progress: she sits on a side table, raising a glass to the lens, and a cigarette hangs down from her ruby lips. Her hair is immaculately coiffeured, she is well accoutred in bling, and her skirt and jacket, in modern-day terms, are definitely designer quality. There she sits, celebrating womanly freedom. There are no signs of unease or restraint: she raises a glass to 'the new woman' who had taken up bicycling a few decades earlier, and who was to do men's work in the war that was about to escalate into the Great War at the time of the photo.

There were areas of work that women were to experience in that war, and one of them was in policing. That was the beginning of another revolution, and arguably, the profession of working within the criminal justice system began to be more visible then. The war took women to work on the land, into the transport system and munitions factories, and into several other industrial contexts. Alongside the public work, the visible images of women doing men's work, there was another British woman: the person with aspiration, dreams of a career outside the home, thoughts of a life other than the predestined one of mother and wife.

There were many professions that a woman of the last decades of the nineteenth century could aspire to: local government, social work, medicine and nursing, for instance. But one avenue to a career was particularly obscure – seemingly a dead end. This was the law. Their place in the legal system, up to the turn of the nineteenth century, had been limited to being prison matrons and wardresses. Until after the Great War, there were no policewomen with full status, no female criminal lawyers, or barristers, or magistrates, and no probation officers.

Intelligent, hard-working women were crying out for something to do, some kind of challenge that would use their skills and test their resourcefulness. In Ian Hay's play *Tilly of Bloomsbury* (1922), one character, Sylvia, is discussed by two other women, and one speaker says, 'By the way, what's Sylvia's line just at present? Last year it was slumming; the year before it was poker work, and the year before it was Christian Science. What does the black velvet dress mean? Don't tell me she's become a Pre-Raphaelite, or a Cubist or anything?' Although this hints at dilettantism, it does suggest that people were aware of talented women needing a professional direction, a goal, well beyond the norms of behaviour and expectations.

In the mid- to late nineteenth century, the woman who wanted something more than domesticity and subjection to her husband, the woman who ached to have a profession and a career, was often reviled. In her essay 'Criminals, Idiots, Women and Minors', Irish writer and social reformer Frances Power Cobbe wrote, with a strong sense of irony as well as indignation, 'It is easy indeed to see the frightful peril to the well-being of the race that lies in the labour of women outside the home; that peril can scarcely be exaggerated; but if women demand the natural human right to take their share of the opportunities … which the world has to offer … by what right does society refuse their demand?'

The answer was that the 'right' seemed to go back to some distant past in which it was formulated, and backed by biblical precedent, that woman was secondary to man in every way. Such was the nature of the struggle ahead so that one day, a woman could dress, act and think like Betty Lindley in that photographic studio.

At about the same time that Betty's picture was being taken, a theatrical producer in Birkenhead issued a brochure of his artistes. The pictures and biographies of his women clients assert an important factor in 'the woman question', as it became in the age of the suffragettes: the respectability of a 'profession'. As Bernard Shaw reminded everyone in his play *Mrs Warren's Profession*, written in 1893, the word 'profession' had been applied to prostitution for a very long time. Prostitutes and actresses had long been spoken of in the same breath. Now here was a brochure with women advertised and promoted, alongside men, in a profession relating to the stage. Why was it considered respectable? Because the context was in the world of popular classical music. Context is everything, and the problems with women gaining entry to the established male professions were concerned with status and ethics – in other words, with respectable professions.

The importance of the acceleration of 'the new woman' in the 1890s may easily be gauged by the vast number of satirical cartoons, postcard images, satires and poetic squibs from the era aimed at those women who desired to be legal professionals. Sometimes these were simple but potent, as in a picture showing a mouse, simply on a white background, with the words, 'Let's put this among the girls'. Another postcard image shows a woman choosing a lawyer's wig to match her going-out clothes. (See plate 1)

In the mid-Victorian period, there had been countless publications concerned with the separate spheres of man and woman. One of the most direct and powerful expressions of this ideology is Coventry Patmore's poem *The Angel in the House*, which has the lines:

Man must be pleased; but him to please
Is woman's pleasure; down the gulf
Of his condoled necessities
She casts her best …

and:

Her disposition is demure,
Her countenance angelical.
The best things that the best believe
Are in her face so kindly lit …

The ideal Victorian woman, then, was a wifely type who lived for her husband, and who represented something sacred, an impossible ideal of purity, the woman's self subjugated to her greater male, the master. For such a person to think of a life outside the home, in the public sphere, away from her destiny of wifehood and motherhood, was unthinkable to many throughout most of the nineteenth century.

If we add to this survey the specific aspiration of a woman to study and enter the legal profession, the police constabulary or the prison service, then the outlook from the time at which more men were given the vote, in 1867, is bleak in the extreme for such a career aim. Long before that date there had virtually been a complete blank in terms of women in courts, police uniforms or in such roles as mayors or sheriffs. By the end of the eighteenth century, the massive period of philosophical and social advances usually referred to as the Enlightenment had gone through its major phase, and there had been widespread debate and discussion on such matters as prison reform, more humane treatment of the mentally ill, and a new Poor Law. But all this had led to, in practical everyday contexts, was the continued suffering and deprivation of the mass of humanity, and women's station in life, except for the aristocracy and the wealthy new rich families, was lowly and tightly defined.

The contrast with today's situation is staggering. In a half-hour walk around the Inns of Court and the Temple in September 2014, I looked at the chambers around Hare Court and saw, in the lists of staff, a fair sprinkling of female barristers. One chambers list was headed by Lady Butler-Sloss. On a noticeboard I saw a list of lectures relating to the question: 'Who will be the next judges?' A female barrister was pictured and quoted on the notice. Back on the Strand, I bought a *Financial Times*, and the first advert I saw in the magazine was for Moreton Hall, the school in Oswestry, with the boast that it had been 'stretching potential-realizing ambitions since 1913' and the young woman clearly delivering a speech on the advert was 'Madeline – aspiring lawyer'. (See plate 2)

We live in a world in which the female presence in the workings of the law is significant and powerful; arguments in favour of that presence in all quarters are indeed very strong. Women prison officers are prominent now in all categories of jails; the probation service has a large percentage of women officers, and women in police uniform – from community support grades to senior officers – are seen everywhere.

The current situation took a very long time to achieve. In prisons, for instance, after the bridewells (houses of correction) were first established in 1555, they were perceived as centres of production as well as of incarceration, and women were prominent as part of the caring arm of the concern, from keepers' wives to matrons. The struggle for women lawyers and barristers was slow and hard also, and was always linked to notions of education and the demarcation of gender.

In recent years, the fruits of that struggle have become apparent in the statistics. In 1992, one set of figures relating to the numbers of women working within the justice system compiled by the National Association for the Care and Resettlement of Offenders notes that 12 per cent of police officers were women; 45 per cent of lay magistrates were women; 28 per cent of solicitors enrolled in the Law Society were women (that figure being 19,987), and 47 per cent of the senior crown prosecutors were women.

Back in the mid-Victorian years, as Joanna Bourke pointed out in her book *What it Means to be Human*, a woman wrote to *The Times* with the question: 'Are women animals?' Her point was that in a Bill being discussed in Parliament, there was this statement: 'Wherever words occur which import the masculine gender, they shall be held to include women.' Her wonderful irony was that she satirically enquired whether members of the House would create a similar statement saying that the use of *animal* would refer also to women. Such was the lowly status of women in society that she was moved to provoke her readers to look at the overt prejudice around them.

We can gauge the scale of the opposition to the notion of there being professional women in British society if we look at research done by Helen McCarthy on women in the diplomatic service. Her explanation of the resistance met as women diplomats were considered expressions of the general objection in all professions: 'Feminist efforts to unlock the doors of the Foreign Office were met with fierce resistance from its long-term incumbents, who were profoundly disturbed by the prospect of a feminine invasion of their club-like world.' As McCarthy explains, 'In the nineteenth century diplomacy evolved into a well-defined career for elite men accompanied by the dutiful and loyal spouse.' One top diplomat even argued that 'it would be damaging to the prestige of His Majesty's government in foreign countries' to have women diplomatic staff. These lines of thought are very much the same as the legal arguments regarding women professionals.

A good idea of the sheer scale of the movement for the better recognition and treatment of women at work may be gleaned from the meeting of the General Committee of the National Union of Women Workers in 1895. Much of this support was from the women charity workers, such as those who worked in the settlements for the poor and homeless, but of special interest here is the presence of professional women, such as Mrs Dacre Craven of the Royal British Nurses' Association and Mrs Jack Johnson of the Society of Women Journalists. The organizations represented in that meeting show very clearly just how much prison work, along with work with the poor and sick, depended on wealthy women with time and energy to give to the reformist aims.

Yet, in spite of the apparent equality in the professions, as I write this in late 2014, the news media are packed with reminders of the astonishing facts that 'Women bosses are earning 35 per cent less than men' and that, as *The Guardian* reported, 'More than forty years after the Equal Pay Act outlawed less favourable pay and conditions in the workplace, the data shows that discrepancies in salaries widen at the higher echelons of management ... hitting female managers aged over forty.'

The following pages tell the story of these arduous and demanding paths to that now familiar female presence in all departments of our criminal justice system: a presence that cannot be denied, and which has a major influence on society, in spite of the shocking inequalities in pay. There are other stories here too: I have interwoven some biographies of the women who 'also served' – that is, those workers in the great law machine of Britain who, for over a century now, have laboured at the desks behind the active law enforcers and carers, but who also operate on the 'front line', as it were, as in probation work and in magistrates' courts. These are such women as the first magistrates, the solicitors' clerks and even the non-professional persons, such as jurors.

The principal landmark in this story is the momentous legislation of 1919, the Sex Disqualification (Removal) Act, which, as historian Pamela Horn puts it, would open up 'fresh fields of employment in previously male-dominated professions'. That Act made it possible for a wide range of quite revolutionary events in the history of employment and status to be effected. It was the first great reward for the labour and dedications of thousands of women over the previous sixty years, including those such as Emily Davies, who had fought for women to be properly educated, and also those who struggled for female suffrage, of course. But there had also been a steady intellectual advancement for such a cause, partly seen in publications such as *The English Woman's Journal*, which had been established in 1858 by Barbara Bodichon, Matilda Hays and Bessie Rayner Parkes, and there had been doggedly determined women such as Elizabeth Garrett, the first woman doctor, and countless thinkers, critics and writers who had reminded the patriarchy that women were not creatures of a lower order in society.

The 1919 Act was not immediately the cause of a whole swathe of changes; there was a dash by the wealthy and titled to become members of the first ranks of female justices of the peace, but when we bear in mind that women did not have the vote on the full scale, equal to men, until 1928, it shows the slow and gradual rate of change in this respect. At least, as I shall explain in Chapter 4, that liberation in terms of professionalism in the 1919 Act did create a stir in the higher echelons of the Bar, and trainee women barristers and lawyers arrived in greater numbers from c1920. The importance of that legislation cannot be overestimated. It would be facile to look solely to the war work undertaken by women as the main generator of the new law; there was much more involved, from open militancy, to the increasing number of men with liberated, modern thinking on these matters, behind the advances of the early twentieth-century.

Basically, women had been gathering and sharing ideas and plans in this context for two generations, from the Langham Place Group, which had spawned the Society for Promoting the Employment of Women, to the celebrated matchgirls' strike of 1888–89. In short, regardless of class, status or background, women had, in a variety of ways, clamoured to be heard and taken seriously for a very long time before 1919. Finally, the Great War and their active part in standing in the place of men in the working world had altered the course of history.

What continues to amaze the historian is that so many women showed such extreme courage and determination in this gradual rise of a professional class. As a social historian, my attention is always drawn to the material, hands-on nature of work, and here I add a personal experience that throws some light on this aspect of women working in the justice system. In my work as a writer in residence in prisons, I recall a conversation with an officer labelled as POSG – a Prison Officer Support Grade. She wore trousers and shirt, and, of course, solid black boots. She only ever really had one complaint about her work: the sheer discomfort of that uniform, and how the leather rubbed, and the material was so irksome to wear. I now see that such little irritations must have been always there in the women's lives: the prison wardress in 1880; the new woman barrister coping with the wig and gown; the justices' clerk or the court typist bearing the backache of long hours patiently making notes. In this history, I have found such admirable women, putting up with all the demands and challenges of these careers, and so much of their experience has been invisible for too long.

Education was, as always, the root of revolution and enlightenment. Women's liberation from fixed roles into the male domains of extra-domestic work was no different. The story of how the first women barristers, solicitors, judges, police officers, prison officers and probation workers begins with the desire for a kind of learning that would cause a profound transition – from the Victorian equivalent of the 'domestic goddess' to the multi-tasking, competent, assured professional woman. For centuries, a woman's education in the middle classes – where much of this professional revolution was centred – was limited to mastery of a keyboard instrument, competent sewing and the acquisition of French. All that was to change, and with it came, eventually, the new women in the great structures of law, in the courts, prisons, offices and police stations that maintain the justice system.

The story begins, then, with blackboards and lecture notes, and leads to wigs, gowns, courtrooms and cells.

Chapter 1

Charity, Education and Good Works

I am quite agreeable that a woman shall be informed about everything, but I cannot allow her the shocking passion of acquiring learning in order to be learned.

Molière, *Les Femmes Savantes*

Important historical change begins with the book and leads to anger in the streets. That common view of history might be challenged, but in the case of women's right to an education and to a profession, it has a strong element of truth.

On 18 February 1918, Marie Belloc Lowndes, sister of the writer Hilaire Belloc, sat with her friends and enjoyed a discussion on politics. She was sitting in The Thirty Club, around the corner from Grosvenor Square in London, and she wrote in her diary: 'I sat between Lady Stanley and Fanny Prothero.... There was a good deal of talk about the effect of war on human beings. Marie de Rothschild told us that she had heard the Germans had a hundred submarines.'

There are many remarkable aspects to note about that chat. First, the club was (and is) exclusively for women, and was originally intended for women in the advertising industry; second, the women were talking about a traditionally male preserve (men would talk of submarines after dinner when they had adjourned to a separate room for brandy and cigars), and also that aristocrats and commoners were talking at their leisure. All these points indicate a new world in terms of many feminist ideals and aims.

The talk they had was on current topics, issues of the day. The women in Marie's circle were intelligent, free-thinking, politically committed; if we ask what had created this intellectual milieu, the answer lies partly in the notion of *service*. Beatrice Webb, in her autobiography, suggests that from the late Victorian period there was transference of the ideals of shared beliefs into a more dominant notion of service. In other words, there was a new sense that serving 'man' – working for the personal and social betterment of fellow creatures, was taking over from merely God-centred active Christianity.

A century earlier, with the Evangelical movement – the crusades of Methodism and Quakerism to help and serve the 'underclass' of the labouring classes spawned by the Industrial Revolution and the great demographic shifts in population settlement – charity permeated everywhere. The millions of publications of the Society for Promoting Christian Knowledge established the place of reading and education at the centre of both charity and reform. When science also experienced a kind of revolution after Darwin and others had challenged the body of knowledge within scripture, in a sense, man began to take the focal position of interest and enquiry. Beatrice Webb saw that service was engendered in the midst of all this, so when women began to enter higher education, and the fight for degree qualifications and entry to the professions escalated, there was already a habit of mind that would relate to careers within the law.

A typical example of this is the work involved in the Women's Industrial Council in the years from 1889 to 1914. In 1889 the Women's Trade Union Association (WTUA) was founded 'to establish self-managed and self-supporting trade unions', and then, obviously, along with such ideals came the tasks associated with helping and advising women at work in industry. The first report of the WTUA covered trades such as those of the tailoress, mantle maker, shirt maker and umbrella maker. Not only was practical advice given to members, but also a course of lectures, and these lecture topics tell us clearly that there was, as part of the Union work, a fair amount of legal knowledge. For instance, the following topics were included in the lectures given to working women: The Labour Laws of Australasia, The Minimum Wage, separate courts of justice for children, Prison Reform and The Employment of Children Act.

In the whole range of social and political activities in this age of the fight for female suffrage and for workers' rights, knowledge of the law was increasingly important, and women were aware of the fact. This may be seen in the ranks of the Actresses' Franchise League also. It was formed in 1908 with the aim of staging propaganda plays and giving lectures and in its ranks were products of the new liberal thinkers, some of them graduates. Beatrice Harraden, for instance, gained a BA degree with honours in classics and maths at Bedford College, and Violet Hunt, one of the founders of the Women Writers' Suffrage League, was another member. Inevitably, these women would learn a great deal about law and administration. This political education provided a foundation for the future openings in the careers forming the justice system. In fact, Rose Lamartine Yates, a graduate of Royal Holloway College, married a lawyer, Tom Yates, and as Irene Cockcroft has written, 'She studied law with Tom in order to help him with his law practice. In doing so she became aware of the inequity in law between men and women.'

If we shift focus to the dominant ideology of the Victorian age, back to Patmore's poem and its thinking, the stress in virtually all discourse on education is that a woman is basically a different being from a man – one shaped and destined for the home and for mere decoration rather than any social use beyond the walls of the house. A strong expression of this is the denigration of them in much imaginative writing, stressing their almost anarchic dynamic in society. In Joseph Conrad's novel *Heart of Darkness*, for instance, there is this:

> It is queer how out of touch with truth women are. They live in a world of their own, and there has never been anything like it, and never can be. It is too beautiful altogether, and if they were to set it up it would go to pieces before the first sunset. Some confounded fact we men have been living contentedly with ever since the day of creation would start up and knock the whole thing over.

Conrad's very gendered prose reaches out to appeal to that construct of the age, the male-fashioned Empire. The male ideology – as Conrad's novel investigates – created war and conquest. Women freethinkers of the nineteenth century challenged the male politics of power, and they saw education, of a very different hue to that given in crammers and public schools, as the force for liberation and reviving, innovative change.

The press saw any educational achievement by women as something miraculous, and it made good copy, as in this report from 1887:

A WOMAN STUDENT'S SUCCESS

> The Great Classical Tripos which was published at Cambridge on Saturday was remarkable for the success obtained by a Girton student. The lady, Miss Ramsay, beat all the male students, she being the only one of either sex to pass in the first division.… Miss Ramsay's father, Sir James Ramsay, was distinguished at Oxford, where he took a double first. The present Professor of Latin in the University of Glasgow is her uncle.

The modern reader might see this is a wonderful instance of DNA expressing itself in the genes of the woman scholar, but in the 1880s it was worth some column space in '*The Thunderer*' (*The Times*).

The early initiatives that aimed at ringing the changes on women's education were always happening in a context of charitable work. Women, notably from the Regency years onwards, being frustrated in the main spheres of professional work, expressed themselves in 'good works'. The evangelical movement of the early nineteenth century stressed service to God and man, and work for the betterment of society as a whole. Prison visiting was the most obvious pathway to this fulfilment. Women visited prisons, workhouses and areas of poverty, hoping to learn and to understand what changes were needed.

There was a more common and general outlet for such social work too. This was in the management of the workhouses, which had sprung up across the land after the Poor Law legislation of the 1830s. By the last quarter of the century, women were involved in the work of the boards of workhouse guardians, across the land. Naturally, this work seemed to many to be no more than an extension of their status as 'angels in the house' as they were still working in a 'home'. But it is clear, notably from research done by Patricia Hollis, that the women guardians were doing very much what prison workers had to do, in all but name: '"Women nosed around (often literally so) those sanitary facilities and parts of the hospitals and workhouses which the gentlemen very rarely visit," said Miss Thorburn of Liverpool.' Hollis describes the 'hands-on' management of these women: 'As they visited the wards, they prodded the beds, had the mattresses picked over to remove the lumps, and changed the linen. Mrs Despard and Mrs Pankhurst were just two of many who threw out the hard forms on which the elderly sat … and replaced them with comfortable Windsor chairs.'

A typical example of the woman manager in the provinces was a Mrs Buckton, in Leeds, where a school board had been set up in 1870. Hollis sums up: 'Her credentials established in womanly work, she was soon contributing to the full field of educational policy.… She felt that it was impossible for widows, deserted wives, fathers disabled by accident or disease to pay the school fees when the children were starving or half-clad.' What could be a better apprenticeship, speaking generally of all such women who aspired to do professional work, than to run a school or workhouse board? It was surely one of the contributing factors to the steady advance of the woman professional in the justice system itself.

There were also, with prison in mind as well as Poor Law provision, the lady visitors. These were the forerunners of today's Independent Monitoring Board, whose members visit prisons to check on conditions, talk to inmates about conditions and treatment, and report back to the governor. In the nineteenth century, it was easier for a lay person to visit a prison, as memoirs show. Often, the visitors were independent travellers who had charitable purposes and wanted to produce documentary accounts of prison life.

Flora Tristan, a French traveller, was given access as a lay visitor to Coldbath Fields Prison, Newgate, St Giles rookery, and Bethlem Hospital. In her summing-up of the situation of English women, she wrote, 'English women lead the most arid, monotonous and unhappy existences imaginable.... As young girls they are brought up according to the social position of their parents, but whatever rank they must occupy in life, their education is always influenced to a greater or lesser degree by the same prejudices.'

By the last years of Victoria's reign, there had been established a Lady Visitors' Association for prison visits, and, as the National Association of Prison Visitors notes, this organization was made official by 1922, forming the precursor of the Independent Monitoring Board of today. By 1944, two single-sex groups for visiting had been made, and then that amalgamated to become The National Association of Prison Visitors.

Between the first prison work of Elisabeth Fry and the first prison visitors, and the new breed of prison wardresses we can detect from the last few decades of the nineteenth century, the move from simple charity to the first hints of a regulated profession was remarkable progress. In the last years of the century, the whole subject of penology was much more prominent internationally as well as nationally. The first prison congresses were held, and there was an increase in social commentary and documentary related to the experience, structure and criticisms of the prison estate. The fact that the thinking behind prison establishment had always been military in hue led to all kinds of perceived shortcomings, and this in turn led to changes. One of the most notable advances was the realization that women should be housed in prisons separate from the men. In the first ten years of the twentieth-century, a number of prisons had their female offenders transferred, as for instance in Lincoln, whose female convicts were moved to Nottingham in 1903.

One of the most informative documents pertaining to the prison visiting of women charity workers is the book *Prisons in Scotland and the North of England*, written by Elizabeth Fry and her brother John Gurney. It was published in 1819, at the time when Robert Peel was in the middle of his jail reform legislation, working to improve the lamentable conditions of local jails as first reported on by John Howard in 1777.

In this account of Fry's work we have detailed reports on jails and bridewells, and very few impressed Miss Fry. There is a noted absence of any female staff, but in one jail, at Preston, the enlightened governor used a monitress system to oversee work by women. The most telling insight in the book is Fry's experience at Liverpool:

> During our stay at Liverpool the magistrates kindly permitted us to form a Committee of Ladies, who are now engaged in visiting and superintending the numerous females in this large prison. It was highly interesting to observe how much these unhappy women rejoiced in the prospect of being thus watched and protected.

In Fry's report, when she puts together her general observations, the subject of female staff is made a special issue:

> Women prisoners are generally very fearfully exposed to the male servants of the prisons in which they are confined. Such servants are necessarily very frequently in their company, and may sometimes be tempted to apply these opportunities of communication to corrupt and dangerous purposes. From the probability of all such contamination these women ought to be protected by being placed under the care of a matron and other female officers.

What runs through all this is the activities of women who wanted to be involved in that ideal of service: the wish to serve, to do something for the betterment of mankind and to offer practical help in the advancement of a society on the rise, which was the case at the climax of Victoria's reign, when the Empire was ascendant, and for generations the women of Britain had sustained the great imperial enterprise by providing sons for administration and militarism. Within this there was the quiet but insistent push towards women's education.

Charity was more than simply an option to do something useful to others; for many women it was the best move towards a professional career. This can be seen in the life and work of Beatrice Webb, as she explains in her autobiography:

> It was in the autumn of 1883 that I took the first step as an investigator.... What had been borne into me during my book studies was my utter ignorance of the urban working class, that is, four-fifths of my fellow-countrymen. During the preceding London season I had joined a Charity Organization Committee and acted as one of its visitors in the slums of London.

In one particular life we may see exactly what kind of quest and challenge this was: the woman was Emily Davies, whose portrait hangs in Girton College, Cambridge, and whose memorial reads: 'Throughout her life a leader in the struggle for the education and enfranchisement of women. By her faith and unwearied efforts this college was founded and established.' She was born in 1830, and lived to the grand old age of ninety-one. After early struggles to establish local examinations for women, so that they could matriculate and eventually perhaps be awarded degrees at universities, a turning point came in 1869 when the new college for women, growing from an executive committee, became closer when an experimental establishment was formed at Benslow House, Hitchin. Then, in 1873, at Michaelmas Term, Girton College was opened.

As Emily's biographer, Daphne Bennett, wrote, what was achieved was 'a family of women', but much more. Gradually, the girl students were allowed to participate more in university life, rather than being part of some strange experiment; lectures in medicine were opened up to them, for instance. This meant that a mixed medical class would have to be handled by the authorities. After a very long time, higher education for women was becoming a reality. The University of London opened its doors to women in 1878; Somerville and Lady Margaret Hall started in 1879. Then, in 1882, the issue of certificates for women was allowed, certifying that they had obtained a Tripos. A foundation was being established from which women's professionalization was becoming a reality.

Yet the aim of there being degrees for women was not yet attained by 1889, when Emily was at an age when many would have retired. At that time, the topic was hot news in the papers. Daphne Bennett explains the state of mind Emily had at that point, after decades of struggle for equality: 'Up to now she had gone forward steadily and slowly but always onward, overcoming setbacks as they arose and never giving way completely to despair. But now wherever she looked she was blocked by implacable enemies.' Then, in 1887, there was a significant event: Agnata Ramsay, at Girton, won a place in the first class of the Classical Tripos, and the university did nothing. Bennett quotes an anonymous rhyme that expressed the feelings of many at this outrageous situation in which women were equalling men but not being eligible for degrees:

No fear have we of competition
On equal terms and like tuition
To keep us from the fellows' table
Yours but to vote for Thursday's graces
Assigning us our rightful places,
Then honour, fellowship and riches
Will give us all we want – the breeches.

Then, in 1897, came the decision that women should be given degrees, but would still not be able to become full members of the university. At least the major aim had been achieved.

This is all worth recounting because Emily Davies's battle provided a platform without which there could have been no progression to such careers as barrister for women. All the professional categories we now take for granted in this respect – barrister, lawyer, prison governor, chief probation officer, judge or police commissioner – have their roots in this notion of a women being able to become a full graduate, and the attainment of a degree stands as a cornerstone of this history. As Emily Davies's life shows, that long and tumultuous history is a series of biographies, all of them stories of pioneers.

By c1900 the charity work done in prisons by women, along with the penal occupations of matron and wardress, and the unacknowledged work done by women in police court missionary support, all come together as (as far as mainstream records are concerned) an invisible presence in the criminal justice system. That system was necessarily, by that time, a creature in transition. It was a system loaded with shortcomings and purblind perceptions; it laboured under a semblance of reform and high ideals, but necessarily gave in to pragmatism and sheer necessity in a world in which a second industrial revolution was grinding much of urban humanity into extreme poverty and deprivation. The social surveys of the time, undertaken by Booth and Rowntree, asserted this terrible shame of crime emanating from extreme need and often from hunger. Women were needed in the work that sustained some kind of bare provision, and were hardly ever acknowledged or rewarded. Everything they did was seen as an extension of their motherly qualities and their caring nature.

Education was the necessary engine of social change in respect of women having the possibility of a professional career. But despite all the efforts of Emily Davies and her peers, the equality we take for granted today was not achieved until long after the first degrees were awarded to women: not until 1920 were women able to earn degrees at Oxford, and it was 1948 before women students at Cambridge were allowed to graduate. In fact, this particular thread of history shows Oxbridge in a very bad light, when we consider that as long ago as 1878 London University led the way by allowing women students to read for degrees. We have to express bafflement at Oxford's allowing women to take degree examinations in 1884, but issuing no awards to successful students.

Chapter 2

The First Law Students and the Women Lawyers

An unlesson'd girl, unschooled, unpractised;
Happy in this, she is not yet so old
But she may learn.

Shakespeare, *The Merchant of Venice*

In the 1890s, the press were worried about the prospect of there being women lawyers in the land. In the satirical papers in particular, the subject made good copy. *Punch*, as usual, led the field. One drawing that sums up how such a thing as women barristers was an absurd concept is a picture of a woman wearing the wig and silk of the profession standing by a shop window that has two wigs on display: one for 'court' and one for 'driving'. The caption is 'Probably the next absurdity'.

When it became more widely known that women had been admitted to the Paris Bar, *Punch* responded with a rhyme headed, 'To Portia at the Bar':

Their trade is legal – so is thine
Yet not their craft thou pliest,
For they are in the liquor line
And thou in law – the driest.
But welcome barmaid, hail to thee!
Bright be thy lot and griefless!
And may thy portion never be,
Like this poor writer's, briefless.

What readers would never know from these responses was that, in fact, the women behind the new emerging legal profession were scholarly types – the best in many ways. They, more than anyone, inherited the term (sometimes derogatory) of 'bluestocking' and there is a link between these writers, talkers and literary types and the future lawyers.

The word 'bluestocking' has a long history. According to John Timbs, writing in the 1890s, it began to be used around 1400 in Venice, when the society known as the Società della Calza were distinguished by the colour of their stockings. Later, the most famous Bluestocking Club was the one that gathered around Lady Mary Wortley Montagu in the eighteenth century. Then, closer to the years of early feminist activity, as Timbs notes, 'The last of the Club was the lively Miss Monckton, afterwards Countess of Cork, who died at upwards of ninety years of age at her house in New Burlington Street in 1840.'

The general notion of a bluestocking is important here because the idea of a studious woman, in a society of her peers, always had a negative connotation, but it later earned a more complimentary meaning when such scholarly women studied the professions, rather than merely attending conversation parties talking about books.

The notion of the bluestocking made Victorians think of the women aiming at the professions, and the story of the first women law students reveals a stunning set of studious achievements. The often derogatory term 'bluestocking' had been unkindly applied to any women who stepped into the intellectual arena occupied by men. Not only had Shakespeare created a character who was a female lawyer – Portia in *The Merchant of Venice* – but in the great playwright's own time there had been Lady Crawford, who spoke for an accused in the dock in 1563. Legal knowledge and intellectual status had been placed together in popular culture for very many years when, in the 1870s, women first applied to be members of the Law Society.

Consequently, before beginning the history of the first women to take legal qualifications, it is profitable to comment on a key work in the subject of professional women and their intellectual struggles: Virginia

Woolf's *Three Guineas*, first published in 1938, when the long history of women's professional status could be viewed with the perspective of modified success in terms of women's actual place in the law machine.

Woolf's book is written as an address to the English professional man, the person who has been given an expensive education, planned from his birth, while his sister receives nothing but embroidery, a little music and good manners. *Three Guineas* interestingly often refers to law and lawyers, as it is ostensibly a tract on the subject of peace, and therefore it looks at political power and law-making – the province of men. She offers a profile of this wealthy son, educated for a profession from the start: 'In the holidays you travelled; acquired a taste for art; a knowledge of foreign politics; and then, before you could earn your own living, your father made you an allowance upon which it was possible to live while you learnt your profession which now entitles you to add the letters KC to your name.'

Woolf is writing long after the 1919 Act, which should have been an effective instrument of radical change, but she looked around her on the eve of another world war and saw that in the higher echelons of law and politics, women were still holding on to a vulnerable foothold. She wrote, 'It is true that for the past twenty years we have been admitted to the Civil Service and to the Bar, but our position there is still very precarious and our authority of the slightest.'

It is not difficult to back that up. When Lady Astor had taken her seat as the first woman MP, back in 1919, it must have seemed to many that the revolution had happened. But she was blocked, ridiculed, and even found men standing in her way within the House of Commons, not letting her pass; she was shunned and reviled.

Woolf is interested in the subject of the daughters of educated men, in her book. She looks back at the previous fifty years, noting the progress made, through sheer force of will, by those few women who were prepared to take on the status quo. With powerful irony, she describes the importance of dress, ritual and pomp in the male world of power, and adds, ironically, 'Since marriage until the year 1919 … was the only profession open to us, the enormous importance of dress to a woman can hardly be exaggerated. It was to her what clients are to you … her only method of becoming Lord Chancellor.'

Woolf asks the rhetorical question strongly and resoundingly – the one that states the painful fact of the condition of professional women in her time: 'What real influence can we bring to bear upon law or business, religion or politics – we to whom many doors are still locked … we who have neither capital nor force behind us?'

That was in 1938. Now, if we switch back to the mid-Victorian years, it is possible to see just how tough the struggle for women aspiring to work in the law really was. If we survey the years c1880–1920 we may see a sprinkling of women who achieved high status in the courts: the first solicitors and barristers stand out, and their biographies form the spine of that narrative that starts with the first woman to gain a law degree through to Rose Heilbron, who died in 2005, having become the first female High Court judge. Then, behind that succession of biographies, there is a series of highs and lows, as individuals achieve specific work or status within the justice system. The bluestockings who had earlier met and talked, used their intellects and pressed for social change, saw that law was the channel for their fulfilment, not necessarily the demonstration and the militancy of the suffragettes, although many law students were also militant suffragettes, of course.

In a well-worn old volume in a legal archive there is a signature: 'Mary Wright Symonds 1909'. She lived in Highgate at the time, and the volume she owned was *Staple Inn and its Story*, by T. Cato Worsfold. This would not be so remarkable if that was all we had from Mary Symonds. But there is more. She wrote other things in the book, including this:

> On Saturday, Nov. 19.1921 we (ex-students) with Mr A.S. Walker, visited Staple Inn. Among other objects of interest, we noted a pewter dish hung on the screen in the hall.

Mary had been a law student there. Her copy of the book is peppered with her scribbles, notes and lovingly written comments on people she had known. This is a remarkable piece of memorabilia: she was one of a rare breed. Mary's notes and marginal comments display a woman who absolutely loved her life as a law student, and she clearly recalled her student days with great affection. Although by that date, there were such organizations in the US as the Women's Bar Association of Illinois, in Britain, Mary was one of an unacknowledged minority. But that was soon to change.

In the long history of the legal profession, and most prominently in the establishment and traditions of the Bar, women played no part whatsoever until the last years of the nineteenth century. Over the centuries since early medieval times, the various categories of legal specialists, from advocates to will writers and scriveners, had been male preserves.

In the mid-nineteenth century, when at last there were serious considerations being given to the view that women might have sufficient brainpower, moral fibre and sheer physical stamina to match those abilities in men, there was the first remote possibility that women might eventually wear the silk and wig, or at least handle conveyancing work or deal with the writing of a will. But these theories and ambitions were firmly in the ranks of the intellectual ladies of the bluestocking circles. There had been societies of women who gathered to have tea and talk about the latest books and philosophies, centuries before the Victorian bluestockings, but, as with so many aspects of life in this context, most men were happy to tolerate such gatherings as long as the women kept to tea and theories. But matters were becoming more urgent and threats to the male dominance of the legal profession were sometimes much less than distant.

In part, this change was because of the Enlightenment of the eighteenth century, as that great intellectual evolution of liberal and humane ideas had opened up discussion regarding the nature of law, and how legal institutions might relate to the notion of equality. Hence the first women who took an interest in legal matters and who considered some kind of law work as a career were very well informed about the necessary struggle ahead. That struggle came from the much deeper, long-held ideologies of male supremacy and beliefs about the essential fragility of woman. The thinking in Victorian times was, in spite of the fact that a woman was now queen and showed that she had sense as well as sensibility, that a woman could not be exposed to the lower reaches of human depravity; also that her moral compass was required to keep the Empire clean, efficient and well supplied with young men who would run the East India Company and the Civil Service, to say nothing of the armed forces.

The deep-seated prejudice of attitudes against women having minds is clearly expressed in Samuel Johnson's famous quip, 'Sir, a woman's preaching is like a dog's walking on his hind legs. It is not done well, but you are surprised to find it done at all.' He, like most of his male generation, believed in a tight social and gender-defined hierarchy, as he revealed when he said, 'Subordination tends greatly to human happiness. Were we all upon an equality, we should have no other enjoyment than animal pleasure.' In other words, any changes in that hierarchy would make us all revert to beasts, and women should stay as they are – subordinated. In him we see the limits of the 'Enlightenment' – a phenomenon with plenty of good fruit, but with some rotten apples still in evidence.

Cartoons and satires abounded, ridiculing the idea that a woman could ever wear silk or speak, as Shakespeare's lawyer character Portia had done, in *The Merchant of Venice*, to win her case against the grasping usurer, Shylock. But as the words of the American freedom song from Sam Cook has it, 'a change is gonna come' was the spirit of the 'advanced women' of the higher-class circles of writers and thinkers. That change would have to be in the very structures of the educational system.

In the United States of America, things were very different: the law students in Britain must have been envious. As women here studied the hefty law books, passed exams but found that their would-be careers halted at that point, over the Atlantic women such as Marion Drake were well established. Her biography in *The Chicago Legal News* of 1900 reads:

> Marion H. Drake graduated from the Chicago College of Law in 1892, was admitted to the Illinois Bar in June 1892, and was in the law office

> of Moran, Kraus and Mayer about three years. At the commencement exercises of the Chicago College of Law in 1895 Miss Drake delivered a paper upon 'The Lawyer as a Philanthropist'.

The same profiles of women make it clear that in the States a woman could come from an obscure background and make a career, as was the case with Jessie Davis, who was born on a farm in Stirling, Illinois, did a course at a business college and taught school for two years before going to Kent College of Law.

The contrast is startling. It highlights the sheer weight of tradition, and of static thinking on the part of the education structure here in Britain. The fact is that the States had no dominant and very conservative institution such as the Inns of Court.

The truth is that through the centuries the legal profession was something from which women were excluded. Despite the fact that there was a clause in the Solicitors' Act of 1843 that stated 'Every word importing the masculine gender only shall extend and be applied to a female as well as to a male', it was not until the Sex Disqualification (Removal) Act of 1919 that all professions had to admit women. But there were women law students at Oxford and Cambridge in the nineteenth century. There was also the option for women to study for an external degree of LL.B (Bachelor of Laws). Research by Rosemary Auchmuty has shown that there were no women law students at provincial universities in the Victorian years.

At Cambridge, Janet Wood studied at Girton (1875-78); Anne Tuthill was also at that college (1876-79) and Sarah Ellen Mason was there (1878-81). Girton College opened in 1869, founded by Emily Davies, with just five students. The famous Tripos examination was closed to women until 1891, and there was a Law Tripos, covering nine areas of legal study. There were therefore law students who were women up to the twentieth-century, but no practising female lawyers: this came in 1920, when Helena Normanton was called to the Bar and then given brief at the High Court of Justice and the Central Criminal Court in 1922. The first woman solicitor was Carrie Morrison, also a graduate of Girton, who was also admitted in 1922.

Earlier, Margaret Hall had tried to gain admission to the Bar, and in 1903 Bertha Cave applied to study at Gray's Inn. The benchers turned her down. Lord Halsbury said, 'There is no precedent for ladies being called to the English Bar.' There were appeals against these blocks to admission, but progress was slow. Arguably, as in so many occupations, it took the Great War and women's participation in all kinds of new work to change matters.

Undoubtedly the most celebrated woman lawyer of the twentieth-century was Dame Rose Heilbron. She died in December 2005, at the age of ninety-one, and had been the first woman to win a scholarship to Gray's Inn. She was also the first woman to be appointed silk and to take part in a murder case. Her career was a series of legal 'firsts' – including being the first woman recorder and the first female treasurer at Gray's Inn. By 1946 she had appeared in ten murder trials, and when she was just thirty-four, along with Helena Normanton, she became a King's Counsel. Perhaps her grandest moment was in 1951, when she appeared at the Old Bailey speaking for the Liverpool dockers, defending them against the charge of incitement to strike. The case was withdrawn before it went to the jury. She certainly became famous and respected in Liverpool after that: she was born in that city, to a Jewish family, and her father owned a lodging house for refugees there.

Jack 'Spot' Comer, the gangster, called Heilbron 'the greatest lawyer in history' and told the reporters who had come to write about him to turn their attention to her.

Such law court victories led to a strange media interest in Rose: she was both a 'new woman' of her age and also, oddly, a name who could be mentioned in the popular true crime genre publications. It seems, with the knowledge of hindsight, that she belonged elsewhere, as the wife and homemaker the papers wanted her to be, yet paradoxically, she was a new kind of heroine – someone representative of a brave new world of the law, which now had these apparently hybrid figures in its ranks. The journalists found her life and work fascinating, but they made her achievements in court often secondary to her rare version of womanhood.

In 1901, Margaret Hall wrote to the press to argue that because there had been significant educational changes, especially with regard to the School Leaving Certificate being open to girls, there ought to be entry to the law for women students. She referred to the US as part of her argument, reminding her readers that over the Atlantic there were almost 300 women lawyers. Certainly in the US there was a very different situation. A memorial volume printed on the American Bar in 1998, for instance, included a notice of the board of directors of the Women's Bar Association of Illinois, listing five women who had all been admitted to that organization from 1886 to 1914. Catherine Waugh McCulloch was Master in Chancery of Cook County in 1917, when British women law students were still striving for recognition.

But none of this information helped. Margaret Hall herself applied to the Society of Law Agents in Scotland to be allowed to take their entry examination. She was refused. From that time until 1919 and the Sex Disqualification Act, there was a string of failed attempts by women to enter the rarefied air of the barrister's world. Boldly, in 1903, Bertha Cave, as already noted, attempted to join Gray's Inn as a student, but the benchers refused. At this point, it is useful to explain exactly what the nature of that 'closed shop' was at the time. In 1919 (an ironical year for such a volume to see print), J.A. Strahan published *The Bench and Bar of England* – a mix of memoir and social history. What he has to say about Lincoln's Inn is an insight into this sealed, sacred world of the barrister: 'Lincoln's Inn was and is the Inn for gentlemen. It is still the home of the chancery counsel, who, as everybody knows, maintain a higher standard of culture than do those of the Common Law Bar. There is no doubt that the more intellectual and cleanly work of equity attracts highly educated and refined men.'

What, we might ask, helps this elite culture of men of law exist and carry on? It is the support network, of course, and in 1919, Mr Strahan explains something of this, giving us a glimpse of where the female presence was in the epicentre of British law:

> The laundresses of the Temple are a class by themselves. They succeed to their positions by inheritance or family arrangement: the lady who 'did' for me in most of my years in the Temple received hers from her mother, who was my first laundress, as a marriage portion. They are very kindly and considerate to the young gentlemen for whom they labour, provided that they do not demand too much tidiness.

Was there ever such a clear statement of the rift between the upper and lower orders in this firmly sealed and protected profession at the heart of Britain? Strahan writes with a complete confidence that there is no shameful invisibility behind this. He tacitly accepts that the law is for gentlemen and scholars only.

There were plenty of other cases that show the struggle for acceptance in this context, but Bertha Cave's was a determined approach. She was turned down in Scotland, but applied for Gray's Inn, and again was rebuffed. Bertha appealed, and was given the chance (with just five minutes to speak) to argue her case. Once again, she was refused, with the argument that 'there was no precedent for ladies being called to the English Bar' and 'the tribunal was unwilling to create such a precedent.'

Bertha was not the only woman trying to become a barrister. A more illustrious and celebrated woman was also pushing for entry: Christabel Pankhurst, daughter of the redoubtable Emmeline. She also was refused, and obviously, a message was sent out to all that applications were pointless against such a great edifice of unchanging belief as the Inns of Court.

The result was, at least before 1919, that women shifted focus to the aim of entering the ranks of the solicitors. This led to one of the most significant cases in court in relation to the whole question. Gwyneth Bebb, with others, applied to be allowed to sit for entry to the Law Society in order to train to be solicitors. They were refused, and in 1913 Bebb v The Law Society brought out the paradoxical and outrageous legal principle that had caused their failure to progress in the career of solicitor. The Law Society barristers argued that there was 'long usage' of certain terminology in this subject. In fact, this related to the

Solicitors Act of 1843, which used the word 'persons' with reference to a judgement made in the Tudor period by the great jurist, Lord Coke. In that usage, 'persons' meant 'men'. Bebb argued that the word could also imply 'women' and she failed in her argument.

However, returning to my opening remarks about intellectual achievements and legal qualifications, in spite of these failures of women to join professional cadres of men, women had been gaining academic qualifications. In Dublin, at Trinity College, Letitia Walkington and Frances Gray had graduated with degrees in law; in Oxford, Cornelia Sorabji had done the same in 1892, and at the University of London, Eliza Orme was also a graduate, in 1888.

What exactly did the Sex Disqualification Act of 1919 make possible? The important ruling, in terms of what it did for the opening of the professions to women, is in this one short paragraph:

> A person shall not be disqualified by sex or marriage from the exercise of any public function, or from being appointed to or holding any civil or judicial office or post, or from entering or assuming or carrying on any civil profession or vocation, or for admission to any incorporated society … and a person shall not be exempted by sex or marriage from the liability to serve as a juror.

Of course, this was a legal statute, and so there were two following paragraphs in that first section of the Act, beginning with the words, 'Provided that …'. One might then expect there to have been some further hurdles to success in this respect, but there was only one significant point for the criminal justice system, and that concerned jurors; it enabled any judge or justice to 'make an order that the jury shall be composed of men only … by reason of the nature of the evidence'. In other words, nothing affected the actual professional status of women as stated in section one, but for court process, there was still a feeling that some aspects of violent crime should not be placed before the supposedly delicate nature of the nation's womanhood.

When the 1919 Act became law, on Christmas Eve that year, women applied for the Bar and the professional revolution had started. The first women applying later became famous names, Helena Normanton and Ivy Williams among them. The latter became the first woman to be called to the English Bar. By 1920, there were twelve women who had attained the status of articled clerks. Mary Jane Mossman points out that although the first step was taken by being called to the Bar, and taking articles, the trajectory of careers did not run according to plan. She points to the case of Letitia Walkington, who became a Doctor of Laws in 1889, and was interviewed by Louis Frank in 1897. Her account of her life is disheartening:

> I had several offers from solicitors asking me to enter their offices, but I did not accept them, as I found that although I could have done Chamber work, I could not have proceeded any further. Besides, the profession here is distinctly overcrowded.... Since then I have been devoting myself to coaching others, both men and women.

Letitia even says that she had invented a machine for embossing Braille. We have to lament the loss of such talent and academic ability to the service of the justice system – and she was not the only one to have been deterred.

On the other hand, there were a few individuals who managed to achieve quite remarkable things working in the legal system, even without actually functioning as barristers. The outstanding example is Eliza Orme, a singularly impressive character by any yardstick of assessment. Eliza was born in the Year of Revolutions – 1848 – and there may well be some kind of symbolism at work there, as she brought about a revolution of her own. In her teens, John Stuart Mill, the social philosopher and campaigner for the rights of women, had tried to tackle and reform the notion of using the word 'man' in the suffrage Bill that was to be the Secord Reform Act of 1867. As with 'person' equalling 'man' in the previous reference to a courtroom battle, here was an argument for the word 'person' to be used. Mill was defeated. In the midst of all this was young Eliza, and she determined to press on with some kind of legal career.

She became a student at Bedford College for Women, and in 1871, the University of London allowed women into lectures. Eliza studied hard, and went through to the level of graduate with an LL.B. She appears to be, according to Mary Jane Mossman, the first woman to graduate in law in Britain. What happened in her life after that is quite stunning. She failed to be accepted at Lincoln's Inn, despite the monetary support of Mill's step-daughter Helen Taylor, who paid the necessary fee of £75, but instead of giving up, Eliza decided to work in the law wherever she could, and with Mary Richardson, she opened a business in no less a place than Chancery Lane. (See plate 3) This was in the very heart of legal London, off Fleet Street and a short walk away from the Inns of Court. An account of their achievement appeared in *The Englishwoman's Review*, and it included this:

> It is certain that there must be some cases in which women would rather consult a woman 'counsel learned in the law' than any man. There is nothing unfeminine in drawing conveyances, settlements, or wills, or even declarations, pleas and rejoinders.... We may have our Portias yet at the English Bar.

Eliza Orme had gone ahead, with her partner, forging relentlessly on into a male-dominated profession, seeing acutely that there were openings in law other than in the role of barrister. Her achievement proved a point, but also pointed in another direction, showing that flexible, creative thinking could make advances where other gambits had failed. Of course, she was also achieving something that related to a deep-set ideology in Victorian Britain: the notion that men and women existed, as in a natural order, in separate spheres. Woman was the homemaker, the 'angel in the house' – and man was the wage earner, the man in charge who took on the outside world.

Returning to the barristers, Ivy Williams's life and work call out for appreciation as well, when we look at how the first women barristers progressed. In 1922, *The Times* showed that it had noticed a significant event – Ivy being 'called'. The occasion is known as 'call night', when names are announced, and the reporter added, 'The unique event had attracted a larger crowd than usual at dinner in hall. The Masters of the Bench, presided over by the treasurer, Mr H.F. Dickens, KC, the Common Serjeant (a City of London judiciary officer) sat in state at the high table', then the writer added: 'At the conclusion of the ceremony the new barristers re-entered the hall to receive the felicitations of their brother and sister students, of which there were none warmer than those proffered to Miss Williams.'

That phrase, 'of their brother and sister', carries a massively significant and historic force: Ivy Williams was a name that would always be prominent in legal history.

Just before that momentous dinner, in March 1920, no less a figure than Lord Birkenhead, the great barrister known in his younger days as F.E. Smith, spoke at a House of Commons event in celebration of the 1919 Act. He gave his approval to the arrival of the women at the Bar:

> Lord Birkenhead … justified the part he had taken with regard to women's demand for franchise in the past, but said that the question of the admission of women to the legal profession stood on an entirely different basis, and eight years ago he said that he was in favour of women in the legal profession. He did not know what degree of success women would meet with but hope it would be very great.

What he added later was of greater interest, when he said that he had 'taken some steps to see that they met with fair play'. He was aware of such issues as the notion that some male lawyers might feel that juries would be antipathetic to women barristers, and he was sure that if women failed, he would hope that it would not be through a lack of fair play.

The story of women barristers between the world wars is best told in a series of biographies. The first of them, Ivy Williams, provides the example of the academic in legal studies, for she never practised. She was born in Oxford in 1877, the daughter of a solicitor of that town. Ivy began her academic career at the college that later became St Anne's, and in 1900 she gained a second class degree in jurisprudence, adding to that the Bachelor of Law two years later. She also had the LL.B from London. Her membership at the Inns of Court began with her admission to the Inner Temple and so began a career of scholarly writing on the law, including her *The Sources of Law in the Swiss Civil Code* (1923). This writing was done in step with teaching, as she was tutor for twenty-five years to the Society of Home Students. She endowed scholarships, and as a teacher of law, she gave close attention to individual students, helping them to find extra help from specialists in their field.

Long before being called to the Bar, she gave a comment to the *Law Journal* that reverberates through time: 'The legal profession will have to admit us in their own defence … a band of lady university lawyers will say to the Benchers and the Law Society, "Admit us or we shall form a third branch of the profession and practise as outside lawyers."'

In 1930 she was appointed a delegate to the conference on the Codification of International Law at The Hague. Her career was one of teaching, good work for good causes, and of an admirable scholastic life in her beloved Oxford.

The Times obituary notes that, 'In many ways she gave of her best to her generation, both by her wisdom and by her strong good sense and acts of kindness.' It was entirely typical of Ivy Williams that, even as her own eyesight was failing, she became an expert on Braille, and wrote a Braille primer following Walkington's interests, as she, too, had worked on Braille.

Helena Normanton began her career at the Bar at the same time as Ivy Williams, but in Helena's case, she was very much a practising lawyer, and balanced that with a writing career and much more. She was born in1882 in London, and misfortune struck early, as her father was found dead in mysterious circumstances when she was only four. His body, with a broken neck, was found in a railway tunnel. Her mother succeeded moderately, moving to Brighton, where she kept a shop. Helena was academically bright and she won a scholarship to what later became Varndean School, and then progressed to teacher training at Edge Hill, Liverpool, until 1905. After that came lectureships, and she also gained a reputation as a writer and speaker on the feminist cause.

Her place in the 'firsts' of law is assured with the fact that she was the first woman admitted to the Middle Temple. When she later married Gavin Clark, she applied to keep her maiden name, as she valued highly the retention of a women's identity, defined by her name, of course, after marriage. This was extended to the issue of her passport – again, in her maiden name. These matters aroused notice and controversy; it is easy to see her as someone who relished polemic and debate. This comes out in her book *Everyday Law for Women*, published in 1932, in which we learn that since a little girl, being a lawyer had been her dream.

Other 'firsts' include her being the first woman counsel in a High Court case, and at the Old Bailey, and even at the London Sessions. But controversy dogged her: she was such an individualist and so determined in all her arguments and debates. Her work in the feminist arena, and also as a public celebrity in some ways, attracted enemies, and she was accused of being engaged in advertising – something that barristers just did not do. There was an enquiry into the matter in 1923, yet still a succession of unpleasant communications carried on between her and the Bar Council.

Like Ivy Williams, Helena did a great deal to help aspiring women lawyers. Joanne Workman, writing Helena's life for the *Dictionary of National Biography*, explained: 'Normanton did what she could to support other women pursuing a legal career. Of particular importance was her role as a mentor and sponsor to female students whom she accepted into her chambers. Women still found it difficult to obtain positions in chambers, as male barristers often refused to sponsor them.'

Helena was also a person of wide cultural interests; her intellect was restless and her sensibility very much that of a polymath. She founded the Magna Carta Society, for instance, and she even wrote a novel – *Oliver Quendon's First Case*, with the *nom de plume* of Cowdray Browne. She also wrote books on celebrated criminal cases, including *The Trial of Norman Thorne* (1929) and *The Trial of Alfred Arthur Rouse* (1931).

The scholarly work and cultural interests stand in sharp contrast to the other side of Helena Normanton – the truly brave and enterprising element. This may be seen in her love of Italy, something that inspired her to learn Italian and to her meeting Benito Mussolini in 1935.

There are a few portraits of her, widely known because one is in the National Portrait Gallery, and another is available on the Internet: she is dignified, learned and surely her image conveys a powerful intellect and a forceful personality. Joanne Workman quotes a reporter who met Helena in 1925: 'Mrs Normanton is tall and stout of build. She is in every respect the typical matron. Distinctly feminine in appearance and manner and also in inclination, as was proved when she left the group of reporters cooling their heels in her hotel while she walked up and down Fifth Avenue "to look at the shops".'

Helena died in Sydenham in October 1957. *The Times* obituarist wrote rather critically, and with a note of unkindness, 'she was apt to turn a comparatively trivial case into a miniature state trial.' He adds another note, which reminds us of John Mortimer's Rumpole: 'She was also proud of her literary learning and an Old Bailey jury might often be bewildered or amused by a discourse sprinkled with quotations from the classics or from well-known writers.'

Another notable 'first' was Elizabeth Lane, whose distinction was that she was the first woman appointed as a judge in the County Court, and to that she added another achievement – she was the first female High Court judge in England. She was born in Cheshire in 1905, and when she married, she and her husband both began the study of law.

Dame Elizabeth was called to the Bar and to the Inner Temple in 1940, and worked on the Midland Circuit. Basil Nield, writing on the assizes in 1972, wrote of an interesting situation:

> a problem presented itself as to her proper designation and how she was to be addressed in court. At first it seemed to be agreed that she should be called 'Mr Justice' and addressed as 'My Lord'. It was, however, presented to Lord Gardiner … that this was really quite inappropriate.
>
> The first alternative advanced was 'Madame Justice' and to be addressed as 'My Lady' with which I agreed. In the end the decision was to call her 'Mrs Justice' – this in spite of the obvious problem if the holder of the office should be unmarried. 'Miss Justice' does not somehow seem quite right.

She was appointed to the County Court in 1962 and then sat as judge in the Probate Divorce and Admiralty Division. She retired in 1979 and died at Winchester in 1988.

Cornelia Sorabji, of Parsi descent but whose father had adopted Christianity, had an education in India, and excelled in scholarship. Her career is better known than many as she wrote a number of books, including *India Calling*, which gives a full account of her education and her life as a lawyer. Remarkable, and in sharp contrast to the other women's lives in this biographical listing, she had her foot on a legal career immediately. She wrote: 'In 1919 the Bar was open to women and the Allahabad High Court admitted me to the Rolls immediately upon application.' But such were her high standards that she still wanted to take the Bar exams back in England. Eventually she was called at Lincoln's Inn, and had lots of contacts from her student days when she attended Somerville College, where she passed the graduate exams but was not allowed to graduate, and she describes her return with humour: 'It was that which encouraged an old woman who had never been really "examinable" to enter the lists with the young things who in these days [1934] do examinations "off their heads".' (See plate 4)

Then, in 1924, she returned to India to work at the Calcutta Bar. In India, she had early in her life experienced the condition of women in Hindu society, and a particular experience fired her to become a lawyer. She recalls, in her autobiography, that it involved a woman who had taken advice and then left legal work regarding investment to a 'man of business' who had defrauded her and made his actions so legally sound that he was beyond prosecution. Cornelia explains how this inspired her:

> He had safeguarded himself legally, and was in secure possession beyond her capacity to dislodge. I had crept onto my mother's knee and, when she had gone, my mother said to me, 'Did you understand what she said?'
>
> 'Only that she is in great trouble,' said I … 'and even you cannot help her.'
>
> 'That is so,' said my mother. 'There are many Indian women in trouble in that way. Would you like to learn how to help them?'

Naturally, Cornelia wants to, and she adds, 'And that was her secret and mine, fostered openly from time to time, when we talked of careers. I was going to be a lawyer.'

Cornelia's studious life brought her the reward of a first place in an open scholarship, but the authorities stepped in and allowed a man to supersede her. Amazingly, she found a job as a principal at a college, and then influential friends won her a place in England. Cornelia the university student mixed with some of the finest dons and men of letters of the time. Her account of university life is staggeringly impressive: she was particularly befriended by Benjamin Jowett, Master of Balliol, and famously one of the authors of the volume *Essays and Studies*, which had rocked the world of theology a few decades earlier. Her comment on her ex-curricular learning gives us a special insight into the cultivation of that sensibility and intellect so essential to a barrister: 'In short, I was hearing good talk, and getting England into my bones, without realizing how much I was learning, or how greatly I was privileged. I know now that it was this last fact which prevented self-consciousness and helped me to savour my experience at its best.'

She also spent much of her life working in the law in her native India, and of course she compared the East and West in terms of rights, values and practical law. In fact, in a little book she published in 1917, on the *purdahnashin* – the 'sitter behind the curtain', the passive, unseen woman of Hindu culture – she wrote, 'You have the bustling practical West up against the brooding contemplative East. If all India is to share in the ambitions to which a few educated Indians give expression, you must teach your *purdahnashin* to desire the Western ideal with its push and its competition, and its putting values on what a man gives himself ...what he makes his life.'

This tells us everything we need in order to understand Cornelia's amazing success in the law: she saw and understood the mixed cultures she lived in as a child – British, Parsi, Hindu and Moslem – and saw what was needed in a secular sense to change the supposed preordained lot of woman in various societies and ideologies. That took extreme courage, intellect and determination. Cornelia Sorabji had all these in abundance.

In Rose Heilbron we really have a significant achievement, and in the annals of the criminal law in this country. We may begin an account of her life with the story of one of her court cases – something infamous in Liverpool, her home city.

In June 2003, a verdict made in 1950 was overturned. That might not be such an amazing fact, except for the detail that the crime in question was a murder, and that the man who was hanged for that crime was now the victim of what is known in law as an 'unsafe' verdict. The man was George Kelly, and his remarkable story began in 1949, when cinemagoers were watching a thriller in the Cameo Cinema, Wavertree.

As the audience were engrossed in the film they were unaware of the drama going on in the back room. The cinema manager, Leonard Thomas, was in his office counting the night's takings. Mrs Jackman, from the cashier's office, took the money to Thomas and his assistant, Mr Catterall. But as Mrs Jackman walked downstairs again, she heard six gunshots. When she ran back to the office, she found Thomas dead and Catterall mortally wounded. The incident became known as the Cameo Murder case.

Kelly was stuck in the place with the gun. His alleged accomplice, Charles Connolly, was very quick to get out of the building. Kelly, according to one view, then had to think of something quickly; and that was to buy a man a drink in a pub called the Leigh Arms. The problem was that the man was a stranger and he also saw that Kelly was out of breath and slightly excited.

This happened in March, and then in September, when there were no real suspects being investigated, Liverpool Police had a letter in which the writer said he knew the names of the killers, and that if the police would place an advert in the *Liverpool Echo*, the results would be of great interest. The police were keen to make progress; they had questioned more than 65,000 people. Intrigued, and willing to try anything at that time, the police did so. When the advert was placed, a man called James Northam rang the station and after that he met officers and told a story of how he overheard two men planning the robbery: they were George Kelly and Charles Connolly. They were charged, and what followed was at the time to be the longest criminal trial on record.

Kelly was twenty-seven, he was a labourer, as was Connolly, but the 'grass', Northam, had also been involved. Other memoirs of Kelly refer to his earlier work as a 'barker' for an escapologist and even a deserter from the Navy. The situation led to the first trial being indecisive. After thirteen days, the jury could not agree. Then, on 3 February, as *The Times* announced, the two men were to be tried separately. The newspaper account explained why, quoting Mr Justice Cassells: 'So far as I read the depositions, they seem to disclose that the two cases for the prosecution differ in fact and law and in some important respects. A separate trial eliminates all evidence which is not directly against the person being tried.' That time a verdict was reached: guilty. There was a murder charge against Kelly and his sentence was death. Connolly received only a ten-year sentence for robbery. Kelly was to hang.

An appeal followed, and Rose Heilbron, who had been born in Liverpool in 1914 and who became the first one of the first two women to take the silk in 1949, led the defence and stated the case. She was the first woman to lead a murder case. The issue, argued before Mr Justice Hilbery, was on the question of one of the jurors at the original trial having a previous conviction. If that person had been said to be unfit to serve on the jury, then that trial would have been void. Heilbron had clearly done her homework; in her speech at the appeal she went through various Victorian cases and statutes, with the argument hinging on the definition of the word 'attainted' (as that was applied to the juror in question). Did that word equate with the word 'convicted'? William Gorman, for the Crown, convincingly argued that the only cases in which a new trial would be granted were those where 'the identity of the juror were an issue'.

Kelly lost the appeal. The case was not referred to the Lords, and the last hope, a request for a pardon from the Home Secretary, proved futile. The man in that position, Chuter Ede, had given a pardon not long before this, in a Newcastle case. But this time he did not, and Kelly had an appointment with Albert Pierrepoint.

In June 2003, three appeal judges announced that the 1950 trial was unsafe. The Kelly case had been handled by the Criminal Cases Review Commission. What had emerged is that a statement made by a witness at the time named a certain Donald Johnson as the killer. *The Guardian*, reporting this news in 2003, noted that Kelly had been known as 'a petty criminal named "the little Caesar of Lime Street"'. Whoever the gunman was, he left behind a mystery and a mess.

The story that came out of this was that a prisoner at the time, a man called Robert Graham, had been the killer; he had been released after implicating Kelly and Connolly. The amazing detail here is that it was not until 1991 that this was revealed, and that was when a researcher was given access to the police file on the case. It appears that Graham must have spoken to a detective called Herbert Balmer. Kelly had told Balmer in interview that he had never had a gun and that he did not know how to use one. Clearly, he wasn't listened to or believed. Balmer was a man in the centre of controversy in other large-scale Liverpool crimes as well. Frankie Fraser recalls him as 'the most famous copper in Liverpool a bit before and after the war'. He adds that Balmer 'had three big cases and there's still trouble going on about one if not two of them.' We now know what an ironical understatement that is.

Rose Helibron emerges as a charismatic figure in this as in many other forensic encounters. As a recent profile of her in *Her Brilliant Career*, by Rachel Cooke, demonstrates, Rose was a source of fascination to the press and the media generally. After all, here was a housewife and mother, at a time when the massive power of advertising was geared towards depicting women as house-proud little nesters, aiming to please the male breadwinner. She defied the stereotypes, having a large home and a successful professional career. Yet she was also very feminine and charming, and the photographs of her in her silk and wig present to the reading public an anomaly – a fascinating destruction of that figure they had seen in countless old films, the crusty old judge in the wig, frowning and presenting tough sentences to the villains in the dock.

Rose Heilbron was born in Liverpool in 1924, into a Jewish family most well known locally for their Cunard Hotel in Great George's Square. Her father Max was a watchmaker, but he came from a large family that participated in a range of small businesses. Rose went to a grammar school – the Belvedere – and excelled in elocution. That was clearly a useful skill for a future lawyer. We know from her daughter Hilary's biography of her mother that Rose went to London and tried to make it as an actress, working with the name of Rose Bron, and it is a rich irony that she acted in a play about a murder trial. But this didn't work out. In that, she shared a trajectory in her career with a number of other creative people who began as actors and went on to other things. A.E.W. Mason, the novelist, for instance, began as an actor, and a similar case was Dodie Smith, author of *The Hundred and One Dalmations.*

Rose then returned to study, and graduated from Liverpool University, with LL.B., and followed this with a scholarship at Gray's Inn. Called to the Bar in 1939, she worked on the Northern Circuit of assizes. After that she figured in a series of major trials, on a par with the Cameo Murder case.

Rose became the first recorder in Britain, at Burnley in 1956. There had been a female assistant recorder – Dorothy Dix, at Deal in 1946. This post is that of the main legal officer in a city, and the person appointed has to be recommended by the Lord Chancellor, and also must have ten years' experience as lawyer or barrister. Rose would have acted as part-time judge at assizes, and later at Crown Court (after 1970). This was a very high accolade for her. She followed this with the distinction of being the first woman judge to sit at the Old Bailey, in 1972, and then also the first woman to act as a High Court judge.

In civil cases, arguably the most high profile was her judgement in 1987 that a would-be father could not prevent a pregnant woman aborting his child. Her ruling was contentious: she argued that the eighteen-week foetus had no legal status and so could not bring an action to preserve its life – crucially, through the father as its representative. The case went to appeal.

Rose Heilbron retired in 1988, and she died in December 2005.

Another important figure in the history of women in silk is Sybil Campbell, the first woman judge in a full-time capacity, being appointed after serving as a magistrate at Tower Bridge in 1945. The background to this needs explaining: at this time, there were no women serving as a judge in a High Court, but stipendiary magistrates (who were paid, unlike lay justices, who were not) were technically judges. In 1945, Herbert Morrison, the Home Secretary, noticed that there was a vacancy for one of the posts of magistrate in the London Police Courts, and he saw that a woman, Venetia Stephenson, had been a candidate but was passed over. He thought that it would be wise to take note. Enter Sybil Campbell, a woman who had been born in Ceylon in 1889, the daughter of a land agent. But Sybil's great-grandfather had been a judge in the Court of Common Pleas, and even more important in terms of the situation in 1945, Sybil was a university scholar and indeed a governor of Cambridge University. She joined the Middle Temple in 1920 and so began her legal career.

She was called to the Bar and worked on the Midland Circuit, and then she was involved in a number of boards and committees, working during the war for the Ministry of Food. She won an OBE in 1942. Morrison's candidate, then, was hardly unknown. Then she returned to chambers and she worked in a sphere of law that would be ideal for anyone likely to work as a magistrate: she was active in the referee's court, meaning that she would be engaged in cases of arbitration and in cases where various parties acted against parliamentary Bills. Her life at that point would have been a series of weighing and considering, evaluating claims and arguments. In short, perfect training for a judge.

Sybil was then appointed in 1945, working at Tower Bridge. Questions were asked regarding whether a woman was a fit person to do such work, as there would be much unpleasantness – the old, familiar argument, of course. We have a vivid account of life at this time as a London magistrate in J.B. Sandbach's memoir, *This Old Wig*. He explained the appointment system as it was before the Second World War: 'when there is a vacancy, through death or retirement at any other court, and magistrate is at liberty to apply to the Chief Magistrate'. This emphasises how special and unusual was Morrison's insistence on appointing a woman as a magistrate. Sandbach gives a lively account of the kinds of cases that would have come before Sybil Campbell – drunken brawls, vice offences, assaults and so on. He stresses one particular aspect: 'the work is rendered easier by the almost entire absence of matrimonial cases. It has its own particular problems. If numbers are the criterion, then the most important work is dealing with street obstructions.' He makes special mention of the barrow boys, whose offences troubled him repeatedly throughout his time in office.

Naturally, as one would expect in 1945, when women at the Bar were still a minority and little noticed, there were objections to Sybil's appointment. One technical objection was evident in the Metropolitan Police Act of 1839, which stated that such a magistrate must have at least seven years' experience as a barrister. Fortunately for Morrison, the idea of a practising barrister is somewhat elusive, because barristers generally have intermittent work. But a debate raged on, with a certain lobby insisting that Sybil had been selected for the post because she was a woman, and not because she was the best candidate. Morrison had to defend his decision, of course.

As with Rose Heilbron, Sybil Campbell attracted the notice of the popular press. Some writers in the ranks of the journalists were always looking for good copy in this respect, and they had it when it became clear that Sybil was handing out sentences that were more severe than usual. Back in the nineteenth century, the police courts, having no probation service in support, and dealing with huge numbers of drunks and prostitutes daily, often simply handed out short custodial sentences. The social dimension of the work was limited. But in the 1940s, petty offences were not necessarily simple cases of the offender going to gaol for a few months. The prison system had changed also, and probation was well established. The press took note of Sybil Campbell's actions, notably in the instance of an ex-soldier who had stolen goods to the value of just over three shillings, for which she sent him to gaol. Statistics relating to her regime were gathered, and her severity was shown to be marked and obviously draconian in comparison with the expected norm.

She carried on regardless. But after another similarly tough sentence meted out to a London worker, the papers rounded on her again, notably the columnist Cassandra, who wrote, 'even the most miserable mongrel dog dodging traffic in the Old Kent Road is allowed one bite. But at Tower Bridge, Auntie nearly always says "No", softly pushes open the dungeon door, smiles sweetly and another wrongdoer begins his penance.'

By the 1930s, if we wish to have some evidence that professional women had become involved in serious study of the law, and in real participation in the study of crime and law, one interesting place to look is in the membership lists of professional journals. In 1934, for instance, the journal of the Medico-Legal Society (an organization still existing today) we find that Professor Dame A.L. McIlroy had been president in 1932; Dr Letitia Fairfield had been a Member of Council in that year; among the members were Florence Earengey, a Justice of the Peace, Lady Humphrey, also a JP, and Dorothy Johnson, LL.B. Also by that time, women were editing the learned volumes in the celebrated series of English Trials, notably Helena Normanton and F. Tennyson Jesse. Women had arrived in the academic study of crime and criminal law, as well as in the professional capacity of lawyers and barristers in the courts.

Today, women in wig and gown are a familiar sight in court. In Trevor Grove's book *The Juryman's Tale*, published in 1998, we have an account of Joanna Korner, acting for the prosecution, who was 'exceptionally tall and elegant, with an attractive, angular face and short grey hair which blended becomingly into her wig'. Then, Trevor Grove adds a note of particular interest to an historian of women in the law: 'I had her down for Roedean and Girton. I was wrong on both counts. When I got home I looked her up in *Who's Who* and learnt that she did not go to university.' If we compare that last fact with the lives of the first women barristers, it says everything about the second revolutionary phase in the establishment of women as barristers – principally, the egalitarian dimension, after the 1944 Education Act and the new routes of entry into legal work.

After all, this comes as no surprise, now that we have had so many women barristers as characters in books and in television dramas, notably the successful 2013 series *Silk*, with Maxine Peake as the charismatic QC.

If we need a quick glance at the legal literature in the post-war years to ascertain the female presence in the world of law courts and in solicitors' work, then confirmation of the settled and familiar female factor in these professions is reflected in *The Law Society Gazette*. In an issue of May 1973, for instance, there is an account of the annual dinner of the Leicester Law Society, at which Miss Norah Healey, the president, was present, and she responded to a toast to the Law Society. The report concludes, 'she nearly achieved the distinction of being the first lady to be a president of a local law society. It was therefore fitting that the reply to this toast should have been entrusted to her.'

In another issue of the *Gazette* for that year, it was noted that Miss Peggy Wall had spent twenty-three years as a member, and Miss Shirley Griffiths eighteen years. Even more affirmative of the female presence is surely the listing of new members for that year: twelve women from a total of ninety-seven are in the list. Compared with the unenlightened pre-1919 years, that is a significant figure, and immense progress is reflected in that simple statistic.

Chapter 3

From One War to Another: The Policewomen Arrive

For too long, their acts of bravery, courage, courtesy and genuine common concern for members of the community have been unchronicled.

Norman Lucas, *WPC 'Courage'*

If we look at the image of the woman police officer of 1916 – at the very beginning of her existence in our society – and contrast this with how she looked in 1970, at the end of my survey, we find immense changes. In 1916 she wore a long skirt, collar and tie, and a wide-brimmed hat that looked more suitable for riding the range than walking the mean streets. By 1970 she could wear trousers, a fancy cravat and various useful winter coats. Those two images alone show the staggering changes that had taken place over those fifty years or so.

In the Great War, the new officers, with no powers of arrest as yet, patrolled with an eye on everyday turmoil such as drunken violence or streetwalkers upsetting decent folk. At their very beginning, we see a need for women officers to cope with would-be suicides along the Thames, which was a very real problem over the centuries, but as time went on they were subject to as many hurdles barring their success as the powers could dream up. This meant everything from not being able to marry (this changed in 1946) or being considered unable to take a suspect's prints (this changed in 1937). But worst of all, it was the long fight for a parity of esteem with male constables that was surely the real challenge to their resilience and true grit. In 2014, there were over 40,000 women officers, and they are a common sight in the streets every day, in one of many capacities, as community policing has advanced and been prioritized.

There were many reasons why British society needed a female presence in the police forces of the land, but one important factor is highlighted in the disgraceful events of November 1910, when a number of suffragettes staged a peaceful protest walk in Westminster. They were policed by both regular officers and special constables – a strategy with a very long tradition, stretching back to the riots and industrial strife of the Regency years.

On this occasion, the women, who were simply walking and carrying banners, were subject to the most horrendous assaults. There was such a quantity of evidence taken at the time that a special report was published in booklet form, printing testimony such as this:

> For hours one was beaten about the body, thrown backwards and forwards, from one to another, until one felt dazed with the horror of it.... Often seized by the coat collar, dragged out of the crowd, only to be pushed helplessly along in front of one's tormentor into a side street ... while he beat one up and down one's spine until cramp seized one's legs ... a favourite trick was pinching the upper part of one's arms, which were black with bruises afterwards.

No less than 135 such statements were taken. The writers of the report stated: 'We cannot resist the conclusion that the police as a whole were under the impression that their duty was not merely to frustrate the attempts of the women to reach the House, but also to terrorise them in the process.' The occasion became known as 'Black Friday'. One woman – Ellen Pitfield – died later as a result of injuries sustained that day.

In short, what was gradually realized by the government was that the nature of policing had to change, to adapt to the kinds of social events that were not perpetrated by hardened thugs and vicious anarchists. There needed to be a caring side to policing: their job description had to be expanded, and many of the newly perceived duties were seen as best undertaken by women.

The first official policewoman who made her entrance into public life went into action as a result of moves made by Margaret Damer Dawson, who had formed the Women Police Service in London early in 1915. Her brother was a staff officer at Belton Park, Grantham, where 25,000 soldiers were billeted, and it was clear that the situation needed to have some vigilance applied. He contacted his sister, and soon Margaret and some of her women arrived in Lincolnshire.

When two of the women were called to work in Hull, some replacements were required, and in stepped Dorothy Peto and Edith Smith. The first women who arrived were paid by a local ladies' committee, but now, the momentous event happened: Edith Smith was sworn in as a police officer; she had powers of arrest, and that makes all the difference in defining her achievement. These first women constables were soon officially funded from public funds. Even then, as Joan Lock recalls, everything did not run smoothly: 'The Home Office was not at all impressed by this history making and declared the swearing-in illegal.... But with the Provost-Marshall behind them, the Chief Constable and his Watch Committee took no notice.' In fact, there had been a report published in February 1915 that pointed out just how much benefit there was in having the women police in Grantham. *The Times* said, 'In Grantham, a town of about 20,000 inhabitants, with a camp of troops lying just outside, two policewomen have been stationed.... The general commanding the 11th Division has expressed the opinion that had they been installed six months earlier a great deal of the trouble which had been occasioned by the coming of so large a body of troops would have been prevented.'

Edith Smith, formerly a midwife, summed up the achievement in these words: 'The appointment has made such a difference – the prostitutes have found that it does not pay and the frivolous girls have bowed down.' She worked, as all constables did, six days a week and had one weekend off every three months. In her time during the work with the Grantham camp, she cautioned 100 girls, and had ten prostitutes convicted. She retired in 1918 and died in 1923. The picture we have of Edith is of a quiet, assured professional – a woman who would take no cheek from anyone. At last she is honoured in Grantham. In October 2014, a blue plaque in her memory was placed in the town by the Grantham Civic Society. (See plate 5)

The fight for more progress went on. In March 1916, a public meeting was organized by the Criminal Law Amendment Committee. It was held at the Mansion House in London, and the aim was to achieve some proper training for the new women police. One speaker expressed the strongest contemporary argument for the women: 'Certainly women as police could be of great service in certain cases in which women and children were concerned, and could release men, if only a few, for the army.'

That topic had been raised two years earlier, in Cambridge, when the notion of women police had been defended with the opinion that, in the words of Miss Cochrane of the Board of Guardians in Caxton, 'In America and in other countries they had women constables for the control of girls.... The work of policewomen would be entirely among girls and children.'

Just a month before war broke out, the National Vigilance Association formed a deputation that was received at the Home Office. Donald MacLean MP spoke for the cause, saying that, as the papers noted, 'there had been no more successful legislation than the appointment of women factory inspectors and he believed that the appointment of women police could similarly be undertaken.' There were arguments based on attacks in parks, with the view that 'crimes of leisure' needed particular preventative measures. As always in issues of policing, there was a perceived slackness and inefficiency by the public in some areas of crime prevention.

In the early years of the Great War, in spite of the fact that thousands of women were beginning to do many of the jobs normally done by men, there was a view that in policing it was sufficient for women to be 'helpers'. The general opinion was that women could help 'in the administrative work against evil' – and this was expressed after one report had noted that several girls had 'disappeared' from Kilburn. This raised the question of whether or not women officers could achieve something against the perceived 'white slave traffic', which had been reported in the popular press for a few years at that time. The police response highlighted something in the justice system that had been unknown by many for quite a long time: the women in the police courts.

A report written in 1914 by Leonard Dunning, Inspector of Constabulary, wanted more recruitment of women, but he wanted no changes in status. They were seen as a voluntary, secondary cadre of officers: 'It may be possible to continue, either under existing voluntary laws, or other provisions, members of the National Union of Women Workers …' he wrote. In other words, it had been noticed that in the ranks of the women workers, coming forward to fill the more physically demanding jobs vacated by the men who were going away to war, there were women who looked to be likely candidates for the police.

As the Victorian years had progressed, police had increasingly taken over the everyday duties of the magistrates' courts, so that by mid-century, every place in the land had a police court. (See plate 6) In the cities, this work, at a time when there was no official probation service, demanded a female presence. The missionary work was done by religious organizations. The Home Secretary's representative at a meeting in July 1914 pointed out: 'In most police courts there is a woman missionary whose services are always at a prisoner's disposal, but she has no actual authority and can only give advice when the prisoner chooses to seek it. There is also a woman assistant, whose duty it is to take the deposition of women and children in certain cases.' (See plate 7)

This was an outrageous situation. At a time when there was such a clamour for women police, here was the Home Office admitting that serious and important matters in a criminal court were being left to amateurs – people without authority. Also, by 1914 there had been a probation service in operation for six years, yet still there were 'woman assistants' involved in court process. In fact, as early as 1883, the Metropolitan Police had employed women to act as visitors to work with women offenders. For a long time there had been a number of charitable groups that had tried to help prisoners on release, most known as Prisoners' Aid Societies, but of the various supportive measures taken as an official measure, the most active were the initiatives involving women. For instance, in 1889 a group of fourteen women were given work as police matrons, and these added to the work of the police court missionaries by being given roles helping women and children in the lower courts. There was widespread dissent about any women working in situations where people swore, drank and behaved unacceptably. But at least these steps were first steps in reform.

Lady Nott-Bower, whose husband had been Commissioner of the City of London Police, broadened the area of concern in the Guildhall meeting of 1916. The reporter for *The Times* noted that she said 'that criminal statistics showed how many were the offences against women and children that men could not and ought not be able to investigate. It was a crime and a blunder to put a young child in court with only men to ask her questions.'

Margaret Damer Dawson emerges from these early wartime days of the women police as a hero. In October 1916 she gave a speech at which she presented a really positive view of the work she and her officers were doing. She said that when she began, the Commissioner of the Metropolitan Police had said she would be 'knocked on the head', and he added, 'You surely don't expect me to look after a lot of women?' Margaret's defence was simple and forthright, and made the reporter summarize her words in this way: 'They trained themselves, with the result that their status was now very different from what it was then, and they could now promise work to hundreds of women throughout the country.'

Soon they were proving exactly what they could do. Just before Christmas 1918, for instance, Lena Campbell of the Women's Police was on duty in the Strand when she saw a drunken man talking to two women. When Lena asked the women to walk on and give her time to talk to the drunk alone, the man cracked her across the face. She reprimanded him, and that made matters worse, because he then punched her in the face again and she fell backwards. The man then went into a mad frenzy, and when an inspector of the Women's Police came and intervened, she was bitten on the chest by him. He then ranted and raved. He was a Canadian soldier called Charles O'Malley, and after arrest he claimed that he had taken medication for a condition, and had then drunk too much whisky. He was given six weeks' hard labour by the judge, and in court, a senior Canadian officer praised the work of the women officers. This type of incident was a regular occurrence of course – something the police had always dealt with routinely. In a sense, the new women police were being 'blooded', so to speak.

Another factor was that at this time the policeman's lot was 'not a happy one', in the words of W.S. Gilbert. In the last year of the war a strike was brewing. There had been a Police and Prison Officers' Union since 1913 but the notion of the police being able to strike split opinion. The fact is, as C.H. Rolph, a serving officer at the time, explains: 'The top rate of pay for a constable was forty-eight shillings a week, and he was far behind the average wage of an unskilled labourer. His hard-won 'weekly rest day' (made statutory in 1910 after years of campaigning) was withdrawn at the outbreak of the war.'

Deeply entrenched in the growing grievances was the rule of 'no confering'. Policemen were not supposed to engage in discussion with regard to conditions of service, nor to air grievances. This sense of isolation in the ranks, a sense that nothing could be talked about and that all discipline should be accepted without dialogue, was to create the circumstance that nurtured the leader of the first union agitation: John Syme. He had been involved in a case in which he defended two constables in his division and was reprimanded for his care. He did not take that lying down, and the argument ended with his first being transferred and then sacked. Syme was a meticulous man, and early in his career had been arguably a 'barrack-room lawyer' because he knew the regulations and related legislation on police work very well. The man he confronted and who sacked him was Sir Edward Henry, a former inspector general of the Bengal Police who was commissioner of the Metropolitan force at this time.

Syme met the editor of the *Police Review*, John Kempster, and an alliance was formed that was to lead to the clandestine first phase of what would become two police strikes – in 1918 and 1919. Strictly by the criminal law codification, these acts were mutinous, and of course the demonstrations and strike happened when Britain was at war, so the repercussions were profoundly influential on the state of the realm while manpower was being sapped over in the trenches of the Western Front. Nott-Bower, the City commissioner, lost a son in that war, and he was certainly in no mood to consider compromise when his men joined in the first strike. It was a case of Syme's personal grievance becoming a catalyst to bring out the other discontents and grudges brooding in the force, long-standing and often rankling under the enforced discipline of daily work.

The *Police Review* had been in existence for many years, and one of its functions was to give some kind of outlet to the complaints of police work. Constables could write, anonymously, to the editor, and their letters would be printed, thus airing certain disgruntled viewpoints and offering at least one way of expressing these things. The journal was popular for other reasons; it was a voice of the profession and it carried informative features. But when Syme met Kempster, and other men were gathered around, notably J.R. Penfold and Mackenzie Bell (a Liberal politician), the notion of a union gained strength and support. There was some support in Parliament, despite the deeply held notions of police exceptionalism in that respect: Ramsay MacDonald in 1907 and Philip Snowden in 1914 had both spoken in Westminster in support of the idea.

When it came to the dismissal of a policeman for being involved in the union (then known as the National Union of Police and Prison Officers), the inevitable happened and there was a call to strike. The numbers of officers in the union was over 4,000 – a number grossly underestimated by the top brass in the police at the time. In fact, there was a certain complacency and inaction on the part of the leaders; they thought of John Syme as a crank who occasionally irritated them and perhaps never really thought that he would achieve anything. But there was an advert in

Police Review listing the union officials (despite the fact that Kempster himself did not agree with the concept of a union). When Syme was imprisoned in Wormwood Scrubs for libel, it must have seemed as though the strike would never happen, but in the months following the appointment of a new Home Secretary, Sir George Cave, in spite of a plan to have war widows of dead officers receive a ten-shillings a week payment, the trigger to strike happened. This was in the case of PC Tommy Thiel, a man very popular in the force who believed in the union and who had been encouraging union growth in Manchester. He had been reprimanded for that, and was called to Scotland Yard to face the music. He was dismissed from the force.

James Marston addressed a meeting at the Pimlico Mission Hall and stressed that the time for discussion was long past. A strike was called to begin at midnight on 29 August 1918. Strike headquarters were set up in Cadogan Place and matters progressed. Troops were called out to guard important locations and issues such as the use of special constables emerged, but it was decided that such a move would incite possibly uncontainable confrontation and that was not done, though there were isolated incidents.

Within days, Marston talked to a mass meeting at Tower Hill and announced that the City Police were joining the strike. That meant that 6,000 policemen were on strike.

After a month of the strike, the issue of the City Specials moved into centre stage. It is significant that they felt similar pressures and had complaints, as one anonymous correspondent to *The Times* wrote in September:

> Unlike their confreres in the metropolitan areas, who live close to their homes, City specials have to provide meals entirely at their own expense, which, together with travelling expenses, means a considerable outlay in the course of a year.... During the last four years the authorities have supplied one uniform, including an overcoat, one pair of boots and fifteen shillings towards a second pair, the latter allowance being quite inadequate

> … such parsimony seems incredible when associated with the greatest City in the world.

The idea of the police union being recognized was a complete anathema. But Lloyd George agreed to meet with representatives, and various groups gathered at important locations so that their discontent was visible for all to see as they went about their business. The City officers assembled by the Royal Exchange and then a large group began the walk to Whitehall, but only after being reminded that they were 'gentlemen'.

This was the immediate background to the arrival of the first women police. Obviously, there was something more pressing in the war years than whether or not women officers should be sworn in: the entire professional self-esteem of the country's constabulary was in a maelstrom of violent confrontation.

From around the same period, women officers began to be employed in the British Transport Police. Developing in parallel with the mainstream constabulary, there had been the special forces who worked on docks and on railways. In the Great War their work took on a particularly important responsibility when espionage networks began to work on the coasts and at docks. Early in 1914, the Great Eastern Railway employed women police, and others also were taken on to work in provincial railways. They were sworn in, and the first four women were given that status on 20 December 1917. By the last months of the war there were seventeen such women officers.

The official website of the British Transport Police explains: 'Exact numbers and duties of railway policewomen are unknown. It is likely they provided a full range of policing services and were thought to be particularly useful in dealing with female offenders and victims. They could go in ladies' toilets and waiting rooms and could obtain statements from victims in women's hospital wards where men were not allowed.'

The demands for a full official status for women went on after the war. To mark the fourth anniversary of the women police, there was a dinner given at the Lyceum Club, at which the two women who were most vociferous on behalf of the cause spoke passionately. These were Lady Nott-Bower and Margaret Damer Dawson. The first stressed the good work being done 'with young women in the streets and elsewhere' and the latter sang the praises of her women, with no holds barred, stressing the training that was taking place. The press reported this: 'They had trained women who had been most usefully employed by the Ministry of Munitions and in other ways in the provinces, but they desired to be more than "semi-officially recognized". They had trained some 2,000 women for the work and had ceased to be a mere philanthropic organization dependent on charity.' Margaret ended with a strong insistence on proper validation: 'It was time that the country realized their use and that they were recognized by the Home Office.'

After all, there had been moves made in a wider sphere regarding women working as police officers. In 1915 the International Association of Women Police had been established, and in the US a similar group was formed. At the end of the war and immediately afterwards, women police patrols were becoming a more regular sight around London, but changes were being rung across Britain in this respect. In Bristol, the first school for the training of policewomen was created, and *The Times* printed a full report on this, pointing out just how general the women constables had been working around that area:

> Incorporated within the school and sharing the same office are the Bristol Voluntary Patrols, who for three years have been carrying out … regular beats in the public parks and other places mostly frequented by the young … at railway stations, outside barracks, in thoroughfares where girls loiter, at places of entertainment, in slums, wherever there is likely to be young life.

As to the training school itself, it was run by a committee. They selected suitable recruits and tested 'those who offer their services'.

By 1918, when recruits came forward for enrolment, naturally, there were requirements: there was a minimum height of 5 feet 4 inches; women with young children were not eligible; the women were not 'sworn in';

and there was no pension involved. The last detail had been an aspect of police work that was causing problems across all of the constabularies, and in 1919 there was to be serious trouble as a result of that. Yet this seemingly significant step was all but erased two years later, when the Baird Committee reported on the work done by women police, and this made a special point about men being needed to replace women where there was a large urban population. At least, any reshufflings of police in these places was left to local police authorities. At the time of that report, there were 238 women in the police force.

When historians need to know about the working conditions of occupations in the past, they turn to oral history and the memories of the veterans. Norman Lucas, writing about the women police before 1940, interviewed ex-WPC Rose Ashby, when she was eighty-two. Rose had been in the force in the 1920s, and she recalled that she applied in writing to the chief constable in Bristol, and when she had passed a medical examination, she was accepted. Lucas wrote: 'Her pay was less than she had earned as a teacher.... She received two pounds, two shillings per week with stoppages for superannuation, hospital care, and twenty-five shillings for board and lodgings, leaving very little cash in her pocket.'

Lucas explained Rose's range of duties, and summed up, 'During the General Strike, policewomen were allowed out in pairs in daylight, and when wardresses were ill, they took over their duties. Young though she was, she had to deal with every type of lawbreaker.'

Responses and attitudes varied across the country, with influential chief constables having considerable power to affect the situation. But overall, throughout the 1920s, gradually it was agreed that there should be more women officers on the beat. But there was one great hurdle in the way of progress at first: the 1922 dictat by the Home Secretary, Sir Edward Shortt, who wanted to scrap the whole idea of women officers. There was a row at the highest level, and the result was retention of a mere twenty-four-strong group of women in the Metropolitan Police. Nevertheless, there was a persistent view opposing the Shortt attitude, one that saw, in the words of Sir Leonard Dunning, that it was 'absolutely impossible for any police force in a large town to deal with certain matters unless they had trained policewomen at their disposal.... The women are pioneers in some ways, but this is not due to the war.'

In fact, some points of view went even further, and suggested that there could be women detectives as well as women constables. In a 1921 Blue Book (bound volumes containing parliamentary reports), Sir Nevil Macready pointed out that there were 110 women doing police duties, and he painted a picture of a state of affairs that could only be called visionary at the time:

> I want to have the woman I can put into an evening dress, with some diamonds or whatever she wears, and send to a place where she can mix with people, and also I want women at the other end of the scale.

Macready was stirring up the type of controversy that had been a problem a century earlier, when the public became aware of the presence of plain clothes men and saw this as disgustingly foreign – like a police state.

In the midst of all this activity, from 1914 to her death in 1920, stands Margaret Damer Dawson, as a fascinating and admirable woman. She was born in Hove in 1873, the daughter of a surgeon. She was wealthy, and able to involve herself, as so many women did at the time, in good causes, such as the work as secretary to the International Animal Protection Society. Her work extended to being active in women's rights and the suffrage campaign. In 1914 she was leading a number of Londoners who were helping war refugees from Belgium, and as her education in contemporary social issues grew, as one of her biographers wrote, she started to understand aspects of crime: 'While trying to find British homes for the refugees she was shocked to discover pimps and gangsters enticing many women into the sex trade.' With Nina Boyle she established the Women Police Volunteers, later to become the Women's Auxiliary Service.

David Rowland, writing for the website of the Old Police Cells Museum, describes Margaret in her role, along with Mary Allen: 'Margaret and

Mary cropped their hair and wore a military style uniform designed by Margaret (she wore her police uniform for the rest of her life).… They moved drunks on, visited the families of girls they believed were in moral danger, and imposed a curfew.… As a couple, they lived together from 1913, and in 1915 Margaret made a will that left everything to Mary.'

The uniform led to some trouble in 1921, when there was a hearing, under the 1919 Police Act, which was, as one report put it, 'against executive members of the Women Police Service wearing a uniform similar to that of the Metropolitan Police'. This was based on a paragraph in the Police Act of 1919 that stated: 'If any person not being a member of a police force wears without permission … the uniform of the police force, or any dress having the appearance or bearing any of the distinctive marks of that uniform, he shall on summary conviction be liable to a fine not exceeding ten pounds.'

The defendants were Mary Allen, Isabel Goldringham and Edith Champneys. This ridiculous charade was the result of thoughtlessness on the part of the police authorities, as the matter of uniform in this respect should have been officially settled long before a court hearing was needed. The women were fined ten shillings each, and Mary was ordered to pay costs.

In other countries, common sense in this matter was being applied, as in Holland, where it had been decided that women police decided what their uniform should be, even deciding on the length of their skirts.

Margaret died in May 1920, and Mary became the WPS commandant. Had she been in that court, alongside her colleagues, she would have had much to say.

The 1920s soon brought plenty of experience of the seamier side of policing to women officers' lives. Clearly, they had to understand and deal with all those offences that come along in police work relating to specific crimes, because naturally, one criminal offence tends to gather a range of other ancillary offences. A case in point was the subject of procuration of prostitution. Young girls were recruited from the provinces and forced, cajoled or bullied into the sex trade. In October 1922, for instance, a hotel keeper called Berkley was in court for procuration and assault. He also possessed a revolver without a licence, and so we have a clear idea of his character.

Berkley had invited three young women to his hotel, in response to his adverts for work placements. To one girl he explained that an American gentleman needed a maid, and then he added to that plain fact that the gentleman wanted sex as well from the said maid. After that, matters turned nasty, and the girl wanted to leave, but was forcibly restrained and suffered a sexual attack. The girl finally escaped and reported the experience to her mother.

At that point the police were involved and women officers responded to the next advert, consequently finding themselves in Mr Berkley's room. A newspaper report states what happened when the first policewoman appeared in the hotel (they went separately): 'To the first he made objectionable suggestions, and kissed her as she was leaving, in spite of her struggles. When the second woman refused to co-operate, he bit her on the arm.'

In court a week later, Berkley was sentenced to nine months' hard labour. Apparently fourteen other young women made statements about a similar experience at the hotel; but there was a further problem. This was pointed out by the judge, as the report in the press put it: 'With regard to the policewomen who had given evidence, the *Recorder* said that the law looked very properly with disgust on the evidence of what were called *agents provocateurs*, but that there were some offences which could not be found out in any other way.'

When it comes to the topic of promotion, and to the achievement of attaining high office, the name that stands out in this period is that of Lilian Wyles, who became a chief inspector in 1932, after being a sergeant from 1919. She was born in Lincolnshire in 1885, the daughter of a brewer. After serving as a nurse in the Great War, Lilian joined the Special Patrols. Her staggering achievement was to be sworn in as a member of the CID when the women patrols were temporarily removed in 1918. Lilian was rated highly by the notable detective Frederick Wensley, who was at that time chief constable. Although commentators note that Lilian, despite her track record, was given menial, second-rate chores as a detective, she was valued by Wensley, who was given the name 'Ace' by the newspapers, such was his reputation. He was to establish important reforms in the police work of his time, including a demarcation of four areas of police responsibility in London.

Wensley gave Lilian a part to play in the infamous Thompson-Bywaters murder in 1922. He brought in the Flying Squad to swoop and do a search of Frederick Bywaters' home. Bywaters was the main suspect in the murder of Percy Thompson, as he was the lover of Thompson's wife, Edith. At the time, Lilian was simply a statement taker, but she did have full powers of arrest. (See plate 8)

In the Savidge Inquiry of 1928, Lilian also figured prominently. Irene Savidge was arrested in Hyde Park on a charge of indecency. But she was acquitted in court and a scandal broke regarding police falsifying evidence or giving untrue statements. There was an internal investigation, and Inspector Collins was in charge. When Irene Savidge had to be questioned, Lilian accompanied her, and in the car Lilian was told to go by Collins. Lilian claimed that Collins had said, 'You can go. That is all.' This became important, as an allegation of sexual assault against Collins followed, from Savidge. This created a tribunal, and at that meeting it was established that in statements taken from women, there should be a woman present, if the subject concerned was related to 'matters intimately affecting her morals'.

According to Louise Jackson, writing about Lilian, her achievement was partly also in her role of guiding other women to eminence in the force: 'In 1923 … she was asked to supervise five further CID women officers employed in statement taking … and she regularly gave training to new recruits.'

Lilian Wyles retired in 1949, and she wrote a book about her life, *A Woman at Scotland Yard*, published in 1952. She died at her home in Cornwall in 1975. A scan of the main events of her police career invites the conclusion that she was always in the midst of controversy. Even when she was given a civilian worker, Eilladh Macdougall, to share her work in statement taking, Lilian noted that there were communication difficulties and said that Macdougall ignored her and 'withheld information that would have been of inestimable value.' Arguably, we have to apply a certain degree of understanding here, as the sub-text of most recorded lives of the first women police officers is one that tells a story of male resentment, bigotry and narrow opinions.

The 1920s ended with a disappointment. Lady Astor, the first woman MP in Britain, had taken a special interest in the advancement of the cause of policewomen, and she called a meeting in Cardiff in 1931. This was a public meeting, held at the Cory Hall, and she invited the chief constable, Captain Lionel Lindsay, to attend. She was looking for a debate, and it appears that he did not go, and perhaps he never even answered her invitation. Years earlier he had made his position clear on the subject: 'I have very carefully considered the question of the employment of policewomen in the county of Glamorgan from every possible standpoint affecting the administration of a large county police force, and I unhesitatingly declare that I am unable to subscribe to the opinion expressed that their employment would be any advantage to the county.'

This attitude backs up the general disinterest in the issue on the part of the Police Council, who saw no need for development of the women police at present. But at least the Home Office made it clear that there were accepted guidelines for pay and conditions for women officers, and the attitude was still explicit regarding their use and value: care of women and children, destitution and missing persons, and, of course, working in conjunction with other arms of the system in the context of women prisoners.

Chapter 4

From Women Jurors to Magistrates

Ten years after the end of the war, and when the major changes in women's professional status had happened, writers and journalists began to explore that success, often using women characters to discuss – and have fun with – the 'new women'. An outstanding example is Bernard Shaw's play *The Apple Cart* (1929), in which he explores monarchy and democracy, and in his imagined state he has two women who are high in the hierarchy of politics: the Postmistress General and the Powermistress Royal. The latter, named Lysistrata, who, in the midst of a row, explains her job description:

> Here I am, the Powermistress Royal. I have to organize and administer all the motor power in the country for the good of the country. I have to harness the winds and the tides, the oils and the coal seams. I have to see that every little sewing machine in the Hebrides, every dentist's drill in Shetland, every carpet sweeper in Margate, has its stream of driving power on tap.

Shaw was having fun, of course, but his preoccupation with women in positions of power in society was an acknowledgement that the barristers and solicitors and their male preserve had now welcomed women, and the first woman MP was in Westminster.

The next step in this respect was very noticeable, as it affected the bench – the very heart of the English legal system, and also the court process and the composition of the jury.

In 1913, the Liberal Party's publication arm produced a reference work detailing the legislation seen through Parliament in the previous seven years. In terms of what had been achieved for women in that time, there was little to brag about. The war work done by women had led to such minor matters as the appointment of 'lady inspectors' in provincial centres, 'in order to provide for more systematic inspection by them of works where women and children are employed.' It was exactly the same thinking as lay behind police reform and probation changes. But it was limited. However, once again, the 1919 Act brought about some new possibilities in the law machine.

From 23 December 1919, women could become magistrates, and, if we leave the area of professionals for a moment and dwell on that cornerstone of the justice process, the jury, there is also the landmark of women jurors to note. This followed soon after the 1919 Act, the first woman juror being sworn in at Bristol Quarter Sessions on 28 July 1920. Ros Tatham has researched this and points out that 'Prosecuting counsel in the opening case remarked that he was the first person to use the words "ladies and gentlemen of the jury" in an English court.' On that momentous day, six cases were dealt with, including a case of indecent assault.

Before the Bill to allow women jurors was passed, there were already misgivings and doubts, such as a letter to *The Times* in which Harry Poland made this point: 'Consider what this means to many … suppose the Lord Chancellor's Bill passes Parliament and suppose a case of murder is tried by six men and six women, they cannot very well be locked up together for the night; so a male bailiff will be wanted to look after the men and a female bailiff to look after the women.'

That hypothetical situation soon came. This was in a murder trial: Arthur Bailey was charged with the murder of his wife, and the case was heard at Aylesbury Assizes in January 1921.

But before that, there were women jurors at the Old Bailey; more than fifty women had first been summoned, and the press made entertaining copy at the array of excuses given by those who wished to avoid the responsibility. One woman could not leave her mother; another said that she had to take care of the family business. This empanelling took place in the Common Serjeant's Court, and one dialogue in particular attracted comment: a women who said that she was 'so awfully nervous' that she didn't think she was suitable. The Serjeant asked, 'Don't you think you could sit quietly in the box and listen? There is not much to make you nervous. You won't be cross-examined there you know.' This, of course, caused considerable amusement.

In the first murder trial at which women sat in the jury box, George Bailey's eccentricity, as well as the fact of the women being present, again caused some humour. The judge in charge was Mr Justice McCardie, and he had three women in his jury. His first problem was that there were press photographers, of course, in the court, and he stopped their activity, saying, 'It is a cruel thing to try to depict in the public press a prisoner who is undergoing the agony of a trial for life.'

Such was the fussy and namby-pamby approach of the male barristers that they created another snippet of newspaper humour when they picked up on the issue of the mode of address. The judges agreed that in future, the mode of address should be 'Ladies and gentlemen of the jury'. When that important issue was thrashed out, the murder trial went on.

Bailey was back in the dock at Aylesbury on 15 January and for various reasons, the jury had to stay over a weekend. The judge's attitude was reported. He apologized to the three women jurors for the necessity, and said he deeply regretted the fact that they would have to be locked up again.

Bailey was found guilty and sentenced to hang; there was an appeal on 15 February, and that failed. In his summing-up, McCardie said a few things that were taken up in the press, including this, pertinent to those first women in the jury box:

> At the conclusion of the trial, the judge mentioned a paragraph in an illustrated paper which stated that the women jurors appeared to take more interest in the proceedings than the men, and were very amused when they saw that a male juror had fallen asleep.… At the end of the summing-up, the judge turned to the women and said that it was the first time he had ever addressed a jury in which there were three British women.

Everyone was making the whole matter a sensational one. When the trial was all over, one of the women spoke to *The Daily Chronicle*, and she gave a very positive, sober and thoughtful account of what the press had tried to trivialize and satirize:

> To the many thousands of women who will read these impressions let me say at once that I have never been in a police court before, but, having experienced five days of the ordeal of this trial, I could go through it again, and unless they are nervous there is no reason why women should not be called upon to take part in trials.

She added, 'I am proud to confess that throughout the trial I was very interested and not bored by legal detail for a moment.'

The media prominence of this trial had a considerable impact on the general topic of women working within the law and taking important roles in the court process. There is no doubt that such a powerful and entertaining coverage in the national newspapers provoked thought on the subject. Women had coped in playing their part in understanding, debating and being involved in, a murder trial.

At more or less the same time, women magistrates were taking their place on the benches of the land's local courts. The post was open to them from 1918. What experience awaited them? A look at the history of the quarter sessions will explain. The quarter sessions courts were always the workhorse of the criminal justice system throughout British history. They began in 1351, and they handled every kind of offence and local tribulation that came their way. They were the domain of the justices of the peace (magistrates) and met, as the name suggests, four times a year. Before the justices came concerns relating to drunkenness, pub brawls, arguments over land, nuisances on the highway, problems with beggars, licensing of beer houses, provision of constables, maintenance of bridges and other affairs, the topics changing as the years passed and society had new laws and fresh social problems. All the justices of the county generally sat on the bench at quarter sessions.

Matters were running smoothly through the years until an Act of 1831, which stipulated specific dates for the courts so as not to interfere with the assizes (which dealt with felonies, more serious crime). This statute said: 'Quarter sessions for the peace by law ought to be held … in the first week after 11 October, in the first week after 28 December, in the first week after 31 March, and in the first week after 24 June.' From the early nineteenth century, details of the sessions were given in almanacs, sometimes locally but always in the *British Almanac*, published by the Society for the Diffusion of Useful Knowledge. This publication listed all the quarter sessions for the coming year, with dates and venues.

It was in the Tudor period that the justices really found their workload accelerating: a succession of legislative measures to deal with the increasing problems of vagrants, wanderers from other parishes and disabled soldiers, and also of affairs relating to apprentices and workmen, street crime and the regulation of all local matters pertaining to the social order. The magistrates were first created as a fresh form of the previous 'Keeper of the Peace' and it is no accident that they appeared and were more clearly defined at a time of massive social crisis. The Black Death of 1348 and the horrendous years of famine previous to that, along with other epidemics and social revolt, made the year of 1361 one of the most significant in British legal history. It was followed by an Act that set up quarter sessions the next year. The immediate context was one of the widespread threats of violence and roving gangs across the land.

Quarter sessions dealt with capital offences until the 1660s, and from that time there was also an increasing number of petty sessions, hearings often dealing with many of the matters the quarter sessions normally handled. The everyday offences before the magistrates were misdemeanours, crimes that could be tried without a jury. Of course, they were the place where the first appearance of a person arrested for a felony would appear too, the cases being handed on to the assize hearing that came up next on the calendar.

In the nineteenth century, many local offences were dealt with by police courts, which were yet another form of petty session, but the quarter sessions went on, the centre of the great law machine in the heart of the social upheavals of the Industrial Revolution, when massive threats of riot and disorder were everywhere in the first three decades, in which Luddites, 'Captain Swing' rural crime and the Chartist movement added to the burden of the justices.

We can see the flexibility of the range of people who did such work. These might include anyone with plenty of land. In his non-fiction book *A Farmer's Year* (1899), we have accounts of Henry Rider Haggard's (a writer of adventure novels) work as a justice in Norfolk, where he was an important landowner. He reflects, for instance, on some petty crimes from June 1898: after hearing a case of egg-stealing, in which a man described as a marine dealer was accused of sending a box of 251 partridge eggs to another dealer, the man was fined a shilling an egg or two months in gaol. Haggard's thoughts on poaching gave us an insight into some of the main issues magistrates dealt with. He notes: 'I have on several occasions seen poaching cases dismissed when the evidence would have been thought sufficient to ensure conviction. It is extraordinary what an amount of false sentiment is wasted in certain quarters upon poachers, who, for the most part, are very cowardly villains.'

On the other hand, in his note for 20 April in the same year, there is a case of lunacy. He writes, in his capacity as the magistrate appointed to be in action in cases under the Lunacy Acts, 'About breakfast time on Sunday morning I was requested by an overseer to attend in a neighbouring village to satisfy myself by personal examination as to the madness of a certain pauper lunatic.' He did indeed, and then he signed the orders needed for her removal to an asylum. It was a sad occasion and a huge responsibility for him. He adds, 'It seems that it was not considered advisable that the patient should remain longer out of proper control, so, as she could not be removed without a magistrate's order, I was followed to the church.'

The justices had a massive amount of responsibility before them and they had to deal with several issues related to non-judicial duties as well as the criminal cases needing due process of law.

What matters were dealt with? This could include assessments of property, highway maintenance fines, repairs of bridges, issues relating to parish constables, financial accounts of various people in office, appeals against assessments, and until the Municipal Corporations Act of 1835, other business would include supervising boards of health, poor law unions and town councils. The non-judicial duties retained after that were mainly of licensing premises, arbitrating in master and servant disputes, supervising county rates, the sale of coals, bread and flour regulations and ensuring that friendly societies and trade unions (in the latter case with adaptations as such unions became legal).

In 1910, there was an advisory committee on the appointment of justices of the peace, and the Liberal government had taken an interest in the whole matter, cancelling the property qualification for a JP, for instance, in the 1906 Justices of the Peace Act; but again, it was the 1919 Act that allowed women to be appointed. There was a clamour for further reform after the 1910 committee reported, and the new thinking related to the creation of local committees, working in an advisory capacity. As Esther Moir summed up in her account of the magistracy: 'By the end of 1911, the majority of counties had established committees consisting of five or six members appointed by the Lord Lieutenant, who was not necessarily included himself.'

The 1919 Act incorporated this new thinking and so the office was opened up to women, and also, as the appointment process was modernized, there was more thought given to how the justices' powers were applied at a local level, and more importantly, there was a new openness to such issues as the female presence in juvenile courts. It took a longer time still before reforms were made in that arena, but by the 1948 Criminal Justice Act, for instance, thought had been given to appeals in juvenile cases, resulting in this:

> in appointing members of the committee, quarter sessions shall, so far as practicable, select justices having special qualifications for the hearing

of appeals, including justices specially qualified for dealing with Juvenile cases.

The very first woman in the role was Ada Summers, who was mayor of Stalybridge, and the role of chairman of the local bench was already officially part of the duties of a mayor at the time. Ada Summers was wealthy: she was the widow of John Summers, who was owner of the local ironworks; he died in 1910.

Ada was born in Oldham in 1861, the daughter of a mill owner. In Stalybridge she was a Liberal and she was to have a very long career serving her locality on the council. She became known as 'The Lady Bountiful' as a result of her passion for good works and charity. These generous initiatives included a school for the education of mothers, and this was to become a centre for child welfare. At Christmas, Ada gave presents for local children and paid for a tree to be set up. She even established a centre for the unemployed. Establishments of an even larger scale followed: a nurses' home in 1926, funds given to the local infirmary, and a number of leisure and recreation activities for women and children.

Her work in the administration of crime and the local elements in the criminal justice system was just as impressive: she was involved in the probation and police court functions close to home.

She died in 1944, and there was a service at Mottram church. Fittingly, there is today a blue plaque in her memory at Stalybridge Civic Hall.

After Ada Summers, there were several other magistrate appointments for women. Three were appointed in the County of London, one of which was the socialist writer Beatrice Webb; the others were Margaret Hannah and Gertrude Tickwell. There were three more in the regions: Margaret Lloyd George, Mary Ward and Edith, Marchioness of Londonderry. In the five years after 1919, there were 1,200 women appointed to Commissions. Just after the end of the Second World War, the Magistrates' Association advised that every local bench across the land should have its quota of women members.

For a detailed account of what it meant to be a women magistrate in the 1920s, we may turn to the life and career of Barbara Wootton. She began her work on the bench in 1926, and the experience of her first day was a shock:

> It happened to be a licensing session, and one of the items of business to be transacted before we went into court was to select two justices to inspect the licensed premises in our area.... Only then did I discover that one of them was the colleague sitting next to me who, when he came in, had asked me to guide his hand to the correct place ... as he was blind.

Barbara served for forty years as a magistrate. In her autobiography *In a World I never Made*, she gives a long analysis of the workings of the magistrates' court, and in particular, of juvenile courts, which were her special interest. She offers a critique of the system as it had been throughout her active years, and she looks back from the standpoint of c1960. One of her main concerns was for much of the crime concerned with juveniles that there should be solutions and sanctions created within the educational, rather than in the justice system: 'I would hope ... the day will come when the social and moral training of all children will be regarded as a matter of educational, not penal, concern.'

Barbara Wootton was a member of several Royal Commissions too, including one concerned with penal reform. She had a wide and deep knowledge of the law, and was a great believer in those whose task it was to apply the law in courts being aware of the actual daily issues concerned with crime. In her work in the courts, as in her responsibilities in social welfare work and in sociological teaching, she had an aversion to humbug and ritual. She wrote: 'I should like also to see the end of all the wigs and gowns that are now paraded in the higher courts. Today the effect of these is comic rather than dignified. Moreover, the archaic appearance of judges and counsel has the effect of disassociating the ordinary public from the administration of justice, and simply emphasizes the difference between "them" and "us".'

She reiterates this in her final summing-up on her life. She writes there that she worked to keep 'the centre sufficiently sensitive to the realities of life', and concludes, 'I have always tried to exercise some function – whether as magistrate, or as arbitrator or in the adjudication of claims … or national assistance … which involves first-hand experience of the impact of social policy upon the lives of ordinary men and women.'

In the decades immediately after the Second World War, there was, as might be expected, some debate and discussion on the subject of women magistrates, as they became more common. A writer who had worked for a long time as a justices' clerk wrote an account of this, and it looks at both sides of the issue. Ernest Pettifer, whose book *The Court is Sitting*, gives a full account of the duties involved in being a clerk to the justices in the West Riding quarter sessions. He gives the case for the defence first, responding to the notion that such work was for men only:

> It is a definite fact that these misgivings have been proved to be quite unfounded, and that the women Justices have shown that they bring to the difficult and perplexing work of the Courts not only the faculties of restraint, calm judgement and essential fairness which are possessed by the men, but also an understanding and sympathy, particularly in cases in which children are involved, which have broadened and strengthened the judicial equipment of the Benches as a whole.

The opposite view had been expressed by an anonymous author, styled 'solicitor' in the 1940s, who wrote, 'Women magistrates are especially bad in dealing with matrimonial and affiliation cases. As a rule they have either a violent prejudice against their own sex or else they think the sole purpose of their being put on the bench is that they make separation and affiliation orders for the benefit of women and girls.'

Pettifer agrees with Barbara Wootton in his positive account of the good effects of the changes in the composition of the bench in his lifetime: 'A bench today represents all types of experience, and the fact that it includes men and women who are, or have been, engaged in manual work and have known poverty … is a tremendous asset to their fellow justices.'

Pettifer was writing just after the 1948 report of the Royal Commission on justices of the peace, and that work concluded: 'All the witnesses have agreed that women have proved themselves to be a most valuable addition to the bench, and there are many cases in which the presence of a woman is particularly desirable. It is, for instance, noticeable that children and women giving evidence often appear to speak more freely to a woman.… There are divisions in which it is desirable that there should be more women justices, but these of course must be selected for their general suitability and not merely because they are women.'

Chapter 5

Behind Prison Walls

They held themselves very upright, and their general bearing brought to my mind certain types of the chaperon's bench at court balls.

Constance Lytton, *Prisons and Prisoners*

The words 'women' and 'prison' have never sat easily together in any context. In the first years of the twenty-first century, Baroness Corston reported on British prisons for women and concluded that they should be abolished, that alternatives to custodial sentences for women should be found, and the whole system rethought and revised. That might be an extreme view, but it does reflect the long-standing sense that to lock up a woman causes more problems than it solves. It deprives children of motherly love and attention and destabilizes the family unit. That line of thought is hard to resist and refute, but in the early days of prison, punishment and retribution were to the forefront of attitudes. Hence the early phase of women working in prisons is a very sad and distressing subject to contemplate, particularly when it is recalled that capital punishment was common for infanticide throughout the greater part of the period up to c1870.

Since the very first dungeons in county sheriffs' secure jails and castles, there was a need for women workers – largely as cooks and domestic workers – but it took several centuries before even such a basic office as 'matron' was conceived, despite the fact that the keepers' wives had been, in many cases, matrons without the actual terminology of office. Any visitor to a prison today will see a notably large proportion of women prison officers walking the wings, yet a hundred years ago, their equivalents were 'wardresses' and were very much secondary figures, found only in women's prisons. Even then, they were not in any roles other than what would today be termed 'support' capacities. (See plate 9)

Prison officers, from the first 'turnkeys' to the 'wardens' of later times, have always been regaled with nicknames. These names give insights into the profession, of course. The prison officer came to be called a 'screw' after the introduction of the crank, which was a device fixed to the outside wall of a cell, fitted through to the inside, where the luckless inmate had to turn so many revolutions of the handle; his role was to tighten the screw and make turning the handle more demanding and exhausting. Today, 'screw' is the dominant term, and it raises the question as to whether or not the woman officer is also a screw. Clearly, it is a generic term, and in many cases she is a screw, but such is the strange morality of jailbirds that a politeness regarding women inside is applied, and 'screw' has other connotations. Hence, 'woman officer' might more often be found.

The word screw has led to rhyming slang terms, such as 'flue' and 'four by two', but there have been alternatives from as far back as the nineteenth century, such as 'dub-cull' or 'dub-cove'. Then came 'jigger' and 'twister', the first relating to a dark cellar and the second to the keys carried.

In the twentieth-century, along came such words for officers as 'skip', 'pokey' and 'bush pig'. But interestingly, women officers appear to have no generally applied slang term for their occupation, and behind that lies a tale – a story of the gradual emergence of the female prison officer from the 'wardress' of earlier times.

Whatever the word stuck onto the prison officer, the fact is that the job is and has always been extremely demanding, in all kinds of ways: the officer has to cope with discipline problems; develop working relationships (purely professional) with individuals; deal with a range of prison orders; liaise with the white-collar management (in a separate building to the prison usually); and also handle shift work and such tiring, selfless tasks as 'bed-watch', when the officer has to give a constant, round-the-clock observation of a prisoner at suicide risk.

In the local jails before the 1877 Act that began the national regulation of prisons, the staff were a mix of family members, local part-timers, amateur medics and ex-military types. (See plate 10)

In the 1881 Census listing prisoners, staff and other residents at Northallerton prison, eleven non-prisoners are listed, and eight of those are women. The list follows a familiar pattern, with the governor's family being involved. George Gardner was the governor – a man who had been one of the six hundred at the Charge of the Light Brigade – and his daughters Gertrude and Caroline were listed also, along with George junior, who was a solicitor's clerk. Only six officers are named: Lucy Norton was the prison matron; John Slingsby was the gate porter, and his wife and daughter, who are not listed as staff. Finally, Annie Moore and Mary Wright are 'officers' and Eliza Topham is 'cook/domestic servant'. (See plate 12)

There is no doubt that British prisons had a definite female presence in the centuries between the bridewells of the 1550s and the new local jails of the last decades of the nineteenth century, when Holloway arrived on the scene. This is because bridewells were 'houses of correction' and their prisoners were a mix of every kind of offender imaginable, along with the mendicants and the mentally ill, the debtors and the drunkards. Consequently, a major element in the staff's work was caring. On the walls of the female prison at York Castle there is an old phrase carved in the stone: 'This prison is a house of care/ a grave for man alive/ a touch stone to thee friend/ no place for man to thrive.' (See plate 11)

These local prisons were in part factories, producing a range of produce from textiles to food. The treadmill, coming into use in the 1820s, gave the prison boards a devilish machine that would be productive as well as punishing, and the invention gives us some idea of the ethos behind the early prisons: hard work and discipline. With this came a repressive regime, with religious worship built in. Women staff were ideal in this work. At the heart of the system was the matron. In an 1850 inspection of Northallerton, the report noted that 'There was much sickness during the early part of the year; this was followed by smallpox … one prisoner died of phthisis.'

The abiding image of women in prisons in our ideas of Victorian penal work is, of course, one of charity and of Elizabeth Fry in particular. There is no doubting the impact of Fry's appearances in Newgate and other places – something stretched into the realms of cultural iconography later in the nineteenth century, long after her momentous visit to Newgate in 1842. She wrote of that experience: 'I first prayed for the conversion of prisoners and sinners generally, that a blessing might rest on the labours of those in authority.' She formed one of the very first organizations to provide a charitable influence on prisons: An Association for the Improvement of the Female Prisoners in Newgate. In many ways, the image of her being among the prisoners in one of the worst gaols in the land did a great deal to indicate to the general readers of her time the value of women prison workers. (See plate 13)

In 1777 there had been the first large-scale series of reports written on all the local jails across the land, by the great reformer John Howard. He saw the defects in the situation: the prevalence of disease; overcrowding; no separation of male and female prisoners; and the particular plight of debtors and young people, who were mixed with hardened villains and so were subject to 'contamination', as it was then termed. Howard's book, *The State of the Prisons* (1777), has remarks on the staff, and he sums up the kind of person required for the work with these words: 'He must encourage and promote cleanliness. For this reason an old or infirm man should not be a gaoler.... He should be compassionate to the sick. If he distributes the allowance, he must do so justly.' The gaoler in Howard's mind is, of course, male. But in common experience, the keeper's family were a real influence on the prison regime (the keeper being the name used for the manager before 'governor' was adopted).

We have a real insight into this in the case of the member of Jane Austen's family who spent some time behind bars. Her Aunt Jane Leigh-Perrot was accused of shoplifting in Bath, and had to await the trial at the assizes in Ilchester Gaol. The gaoler at the time was Edward Scadding, who succeeded his father, Joseph, in the job. Edward was the eighth child in the family. He had been sent to London to train with the Goldsmith's

Company, and was apprenticed there for seven years. He then went to work in Bond Street, but his father died, and the keeper's job back home was vacant. He married Martha Ward in 1782 and they were to have twelve children. He would have needed a large income, and in fact he did very well. He earned £25 for the post, and on top of that prisoners paid fees to him. Discharge fee for debtors was 14s 4d, felons on release paid 6s 8d, and he was also paid for transport facilities at £3 12s each transaction. It has been calculated that his yearly income was around £55 without earnings from other commercial enterprise, as prisons at the time were places with a commercial nature. Keepers expected to run businesses in the commodities needed by inmates, and of course, they had a monopoly.

Into this lively, noisy and populous family came Aunt Jane, along with her husband James, who stayed with her. There was a seven-month wait for the next assizes and the trial, and so her term in gaol was with the family – a prisoner, but privileged. Aunt Jane wrote letters, and in these she gives a vivid account of life inside, with the family. She wrote to her cousin, Montague Cholmeley: 'This room joins to a room where all the children lie, and not Bedlam itself can be half so noisy, besides which, as not one particle of smoke goes up the chimney, except you leave a door or window open, I leave you to judge of the comfort I can enjoy in such a room.... My dearest Perrot with his sweet composure adds to my philosophy; to be sure he bids fair to have his patience tried in every way he can.' One of the chief irritants in the prison life was that the children were everywhere, dirty and playful. Jane comments that her husband at one time felt 'small beer trickle down his sleeves on its way across the table ... Mrs Scadding's knife, well licked to clean it from fried onions ...' With a glance at the larger picture of life in gaols for prisoners awaiting trial for felonies, it has to be said that she had no idea how fortunate her wealth and status made her. She may have had unsavoury experiences and tutted at the lack of order and hygiene, but many poorer people in her place would have succumbed to fever, debt or near-starvation behind bars.

We have to speculate whether or not she went shopping again in Bath. The scandal would have gone on and on, as the playwright Richard Sheridan described so well in his *The School for Scandal*, of 1777, in which Mrs Candour says, 'The world is so censorious that no character escapes. Lord, now who would have suspected your friend Miss Prim of an indiscretion? Yet such is the ill nature of people that they say her uncle stopped her last week just as she was stepping into the York diligence with her dancing master.'

Reading between the lines, it can be seen that the keeper's wife (as at Northallerton) played a part in the running of the gaol. Wives were unofficial staff, and daughters were obviously in supporting roles. At a time when medical knowledge was very limited, and when there were no real specialists in prison work – as there would be a century later – the gaolers' and keepers' wives were often called in to help, and were, in all but name, part of the staff.

The principal matron and her team of assistant matrons, however, had to be intensely self-controlled and emotionally strong, with all the problems of health, caring and diet on their shoulders. In the matron's journal for Lincoln Castle prison in the 1850s, we have a valuable insight into the demands made of her and her staff at a time when there was a really tough prison regime, and when capital punishment was still a public spectacle. The journal is a thick, bound volume, made to last, with a leather cover. The entries are primarily those reflecting the caring and consideration for the weak, which claimed most of her time:

> 1848 … Ruth Buck admitted from the Folkingham house of correction under sentence of transportation. She is very infirm, unable to move without the use of crutches.

The matron's regular responsibilities were summarized in her much repeated words: 'The prison is in good condition. The prisoners orderly and well behaved. Absent from chapel, Ruth Buck, Eliza Dyles and Elizabeth Raby.' But at a time when the treatment of mental illness was limited and often brutal, we have a clear insight into the humanity and sympathy the matron could show, and this is in the case of one Mary Douglas:

> 6.30 Upon going into the cell of Mary Rebecca Douglas this morning I find that she is quite insane and to all appearances understands nothing. Reported to the Head Warder if it be requisite to send for the surgeon. Absent from Chapel – the whole of the female prisoners.

The journal gives us the whole progress of Mary Douglas from that point, until the crisis: 'She refused food … I sat with her all night … she seemed quiet but moaning.'

Then, in 1868, the matron had someone in her care that was to figure in the history of British murders as a particularly notorious and contentious 'killer or victim' debate: Priscilla Biggadike.

In 1868, the village of Mareham-le-Fen, around 6 miles south of Horncastle, was a small parish close to Wildmore Fen. The population at that time was about 480, and listed as notable residents in the 1850s are only fifteen general retailers and seventeen butchers. In other words, it was simply a place where people scraped whatever living they could, many existing close to the level of what was then called the 'underclass' – a term embracing many categories of person from poacher to general casual labourer.

Such a family group, though a strange one, was that of Richard and Priscilla Biggadike. Priscilla was born in Gedney and married Richard in 1855. In 1868 they were existing in a ramshackle hut at Stickney; she was twenty-nine and her husband a year older. They had three children, but also two lodgers: George Ironmonger and Thomas Proctor. The latter was a rat catcher (they were often employed by the corporation at a set fee per tail). All lived under the same small roof, using two beds just 18 inches apart. Ironmonger was in the habit of taking Mr Biggadike's place in the marital bed when the husband went out to work. Naturally, problems arose from this. There were domestic arguments and altercations as time went on. What was emerging was that there was a suspicion that the last child born to them, in 1868, was Proctor's.

Imagining the people involved here, and the way they lived, evokes a picture of hardship and strife. Village people speaking about them later said that they often quarrelled. Richard Biggadike was usually out at work all day, and his wife was left with the chores and her isolation.

This element of the narrative is important: a moment's reflection on Priscilla's life arguably plays a part in assessing her situation and how she must have had to behave in such circumstances. What never really emerged from the investigations was the nature of this liaison with the lodger. His sexual attentions were more than likely forced upon her, of course. The whole social context suggests a range of stresses and strains on the woman at the centre of this *ménage à trois*, and how she would have had to work every waking minute to feed, clothe and support these men. After all, they were all living at the basest level, hand to mouth and in a condition of extreme deprivation.

On 30 September 1868, Mr Biggadike ate a meal of hot cakes and mutton, and these had been made by Priscilla. He took to his bed but he was mortally ill, and died after eleven hours of agonizing pain and retching. There was no doubt in the doctor's mind at the inquest that this was a case of arsenic poisoning. Obviously, Priscilla switched the focus to Proctor, saying that she had seen him put a powder into the food. Mr Biggadike was taking a medicine already, and the powder was also added to this, she claimed. Her story became more convoluted and when Proctor was shown to have no motive for doing such a thing, a grand jury found him innocent and there were only Priscilla's allegations to put against him.

The situation was compounded by her account of Richard having stated that he wanted to end his own life; he had large debts, and she said that she had found a suicide note written by him. But here was a slip: her husband could not read or write. A reported statement by Priscilla, 'I cannot abide him. I should like to see him brought home dead', was the most conclusive point made by the prosecution. There had been violent and frequent quarrels between the married pair, of course, and that was part of the case as well.

The inquest, held on 3 October, heard a statement from Dr Maxwell, saying that he was called to the home at seven in the evening of 30 September, and that he 'found him in great pain in bed, sick and violently purged. He had all the symptoms of poisoning by some irritant.' At a post-mortem examination the same doctor conducted the next morning, he confirmed death by poison and was convinced that arsenic had been used, and in a very large dose. 'There was enough left in the body,' he commented, 'to destroy the life of another person. I never saw a clearer case of death by poison.' He would have seen quite a few cases; that seems certain.

Priscilla had been placed in the House of Correction, where she had a miserable time. The place was reported as having 'offensively unhealthy cells 10 feet by 8 … the only admittance of light is through a tiny niche in the wall'. She went to talk to the governor, John Farr Phillips, and there she implicated Proctor. Her words seem precise and detailed, at least on the surface:

> On the last day of September I was standing against the tea table, and saw Thomas Proctor put a white powder of some sort into a tea cup, and then he poured some milk, which stood upon the table, into it. My husband came into the room directly after and I poured his tea out, and he drank it, and more besides.

She gave more information about Proctor putting something else into Richard's medicine bottle. She then tested it: 'As soon as he left the room I poured some medicine into the cup and gave it to my husband, and tasted it myself. In an hour afterwards I was sick, and I was sick for two days after.'

All this is peculiarly confusing, as her actions do not seem entirely reasonable, or logical. She went on to say more about Proctor, to such an extent that Superintendent Wright of Spilsby charged Proctor with the murder. Proctor stated his innocence. Priscilla added the information about the suicide note, saying that she had burned it. When Wright insisted that Richard was illiterate, she said, 'No, someone must have done it for him.' Most of her statements are very difficult to uphold, and the general manner of her delivery of this material only builds the case against her more strongly. This tiny detail is the one note about Priscilla that has persisted to this day. Tours in Lincoln Castle now have a script for the guide to say in which the public are informed that Priscilla made this 'fatal mistake' about the illiteracy of her husband. But this is by no means as simple as this assumes. Someone may well have 'written it for him'. In the circumstances, if this was a suicide, a man would genuinely want the people left behind to understand, and indeed to suffer some guilt and remorse.

In October 1868, the matron's journal at Lincoln Castle prison begins to mention Priscilla. The notes begin with a plain statement: 'Priscilla Biggadike received for trial at the next assize. She has a baby with her and cannot attend chapel. One pint of milk and pound of bread allowed daily for this child.'

The matron is at the very heart of the prison's most demanding regime feature: the care and security of a prisoner accused of a capital offence. On 30 October, Priscilla's child was taken away – removed to the sessions house across Lincoln. Then, on 11 November, she notes, 'PB convicted of murder and sentenced to be executed … was placed in charge of her in cell 6 in B corridor.'

Two days later, the prisoner was 'allowed one glass of wine before going to bed' and the next day she was 'very poorly and not able to get up to go to chapel'. Finally, on 28 November, we have simply, 'PB was executed this morning at nine o'clock'.

We can only imagine what professional self-control was needed in order for the matron and her staff to integrate such horrendous events into the daily regime. The journal only allows for a bare record: no emotion detected at all. This shows very powerfully exactly how tough and demanding the prison matron's job profile was. On any given day she could find herself ministering to the chronically sick, then supervising special dietaries; this was a matter of routine. But then, there could be the next condemned prisoner, and there was a gloom cast along the wing. Arguably, the most challenging aspect of her role was dealing with the mentally ill.

In the mid-Victorian years our most remarkable insights into women prison staff come from documentary narratives, such as the massive survey of London prisons undertaken by Henry Mayhew and John Binny in the 1850s, and from a strange work called *Female Life in Prison*, purporting to be written by 'a prison matron' but was the work of F.W. Robinson. He summarized the women workers in this way: 'In charge of the female compartment are assistant matrons on probation, assistant matrons, latterly a chief matron – on whom the practical running of the prison really devolves, but to whom credit is rarely given – a lady superintendent, a deputy governor and a governor.' Basically, there was this hierarchy of staff all above the standard status of 'wardress' and we know only a limited amount of details about their daily work. Much may be inferred, though, and we may be sure that it was hard, demanding work.

Mayhew and Binny do give some enlightening statistics, however. In their account of Brixton female prison, they supply a full list of staff as it was in 1856. The hierarchy was:

Principal officers and clerks
Officers in the manufacturing and labour department
Subordinate officers and servants

In the first group, of fourteen positions, seven were woman, being the four members of the school staff, a scripture reader and two superintendents. In the second group, numbering just six staff, two were women, being the workmistress and the cutter. Finally, in the third group of subordinates, there was a total of forty-seven staff, and of these, only seven were male, being the carpenter, plumber, labourer, messenger, watchman, gatekeeper and baker. Predominantly, the female staff consisted of nineteen assistant matrons, thirteen matrons and three principal matrons. We may see from this that, in most cases, references to a 'wardress' were in fact, technically, matrons. Interestingly, the male equivalent terminology was 'warder' or even 'turnkey'. (See plate 14)

Mayhew and Binny provide engraving illustrations of some of the female staff at that time. The principal matron wore a full-length, full dress; a collared cape, a blouse and a bonnet. As with most prison supervision, the work was tedious in the extreme for the matrons. One typical illustration in *Criminal Prisons of London* shows lines of women convicts at work on the landings, and three levels, sewing or picking oakum, while five matrons look on, standing throughout the shift.

Details of the wardresses' lives may be hard to come by, but fortunately, the rise of family history research has opened up new material. This is thanks to such work by Ruth Saunders, for instance, into the life of her grandmother, Mary Ann Bullock, who was born in 1869 at Wall Heath, her father being a labourer in an ironworks. They moved to Giggetty Womborne and then to Dudley by 1881, and then there was another move to Tamworth. In 1891, Mary Ann was working as a nurse in Moab House, a private asylum run by John F. Moody, who was registered as an MRCS (Member of the Royal College of Surgeons) and was a former governor of Winson Green Prison in Birmingham. (See plates 16 and 17)

This contact clearly led to Mary Ann finding a job as a wardress at Winson Green, where she was working by the time of the census of 1901, and where she lived-in. In 1902 Mary Ann married, and she died in 1916, aged just forty-seven. Her husband, William, married another wardress at the jail. There is a photo of Mary Ann in her uniform, with her daughter Marjorie, taken around 1912. The full-length skirt and belt are entirely typical, and the collar, tie and male-looking shirt show that at least some advances had been made in this working attire since Mayhew and Binny's documentary study of the 1850s.

When Mary Ann left prison work in 1902 she was presented with a chest of drawers with a brass plaque on, given to her by the visiting magistrates and officials of Winson Green. This is clearly a definite assertion of the high esteem the management held her in, and it appears that such presentations were not common in prison work at that time.

The governors and head matrons carried the main responsibility. Sometimes we have a name, as in Robinson's reference: 'At Millbank the sole superintendence is now vested in Mrs Gibson, a thoughtful and energetic lady.' There is a glimpse of Mrs Gibson in a report in *The Daily News* of 1874, when a visitor saw the infamous Constance Kent, of the Road House murder, knitting stockings. Mrs Gibson told the visitor that Kent was one of the prisoners she could not 'get at'. There we have a hint that the women in charge were often keen to reform their charges.

Matron Gibson is an intriguing character. She is perhaps the same Matron Gibson who travelled on the emigrant ship *Warren Hastings* ten years before her time working with Constance Kent. It makes sense to suggest that the assistant matron called Gibson on that voyage was on her first medical and penal appointment. The ship arrived in Brisbane in September 1864, and there was only one passenger death (from 253 travellers) reported. Other Miss Gibsons are recorded as working in various institutions, as matrons, in the ten years before 1874, but they may not be the same person whose encounter with the notorious killer from the Road House murder occurred at that date when *The Daily News* reporter visited the prison.

What about the other staff – the wardresses, as they came to be called? It is largely thanks to the reformers in the years after the Great War (many of whom were pacifist conscientious objectors) that we have material on the 'female wardresses', as they were termed then. In *English Prisons Today*, Hobhouse and Brockway provided a documentary enquiry into all aspects of prisons, and they included a section particularly devoted to the women staff. They noted that the retirement age for women should be lower than fifty-five: 'It is probably true that very few women can keep till fifty-five the freshness and serenity essential for the best performance of a wardress's duties.'

The book also pointed out that there were no separate quarters for women warders: 'Their bedrooms are scattered up and down the prison itself, and often at a considerable distance from the bathroom reserved for the staff.' One of the most telling aspects of her work was noted in this comment: 'The warder gets home to his house and family and becomes an ordinary citizen when his work is over; the wardress has her meals in the prison and has no family life to refresh her.' Hobhouse and Brockway understood the human implications, pointing out that 'Consequently, their lives are often lonely, and the prospect of continuing to live under such conventual rules until fifty-five disheartens even keen workers.'

English Prisons Today makes a point of describing the situation at Holloway Prison (by then the main, specialist prison for women inmates) regarding medical staff, and makes a strong point about the need for change: 'We are glad to record … that during 1919 the Prison Commissioners began to employ five fully-trained nursing sisters in the hospital attached to Holloway.' The authors quote a comment from *The British Journal of Nursing* to reinforce a note about qualifications: 'One sister devotes her time to venereal cases, and it is the duty of a second to observe mental defectives. A third deals with the surgery cases, the fourth devotes herself to midwifery.… Their work might be usefully extended to preventive nursing amongst all prisoners.'

Though not in any way defined as prison staff, the women involved in the Howard League for Penal Reform, created in 1921 from existing charitable organizations, did have (and still have) a considerable impact on the thinking behind our prison system, and on the human issues related to incarceration. One of the most influential women in that establishment, and in other prison-related areas, in the 1920s was Margery Fry, who will figure again in the account of the first women magistrates in Chapter 5. Her work also includes prison visiting – in the noble tradition of her ancestor, Elizabeth – and Margery visited Holloway. There, she became the first official education advisor, and she visited at times when not engaged in her other social welfare projects.

Holloway is of central importance in the development of women prison staff. It opened in 1851, and was to house both men and women prisoners, but then in 1903 it was used for accommodating women prisoners only. In 1862, Henry Mayhew and John Binny wrote their extensive documentary account of London's prisons, and in that work we have facts relating to the staffing of Holloway. The female staff consisted of a matron and a number of wardresses; a male warder acted as outer watchman, but the chief warder in the prison itself was female. The wardresses wore a brown dress, with a dark headdress. There was also a school inside, and the teacher, the writers reported, was 'an active intelligent lady'. Mayhew and Binny found out that the pay bill for the staff was an average of almost £3,500 over the previous seven years.

They also studied the Horsemonger Lane Gaol – formerly the Surrey house of correction – and they provided more details of what the prison teacher actually did at the time:

> We were introduced to Miss Moseley, the teacher, who replied, in answer to our queries, 'I teach the various females separately in the prison. Sometimes we have a considerable number able to read. The prisoners are seldom more than three months under my care. I often find that some who did not know their letters when they entered the prison, are able to read the Testament by the time they leave. As a rule, I find that the young are the most docile scholars.'

For a prison with 2,455 commitments of males and 874 commitments of females in the year ending 1860, Horsemonger Lane had twenty-two male officers and six female officers when Mayhew and Binny wrote their book.

What strikes the modern reader, looking at the massive, gaunt buildings of London prisons, is the sheer magnificence of their conception, built to both intimidate and impress. You knew, once inside those walls, that you were in something that imagined for you the notion of purgatory. Life froze the moment a woman stepped inside Holloway or Brixton, she

1. A postcard, c1920, which reveals the prejudiced view of women who had taken the silk. *(Author's collection)*

2. A list of barristers in chambers today, by the Inns of Court in London. Women lawyers are prominent in the lists. *(Stephen Wade)*

3. Chancery Lane, where Eliza Orme started her first law practice in about 1900. *(Stephen Wade)*

4. Indian lawyer and rights campaigner Cornelia Sorabji (1866-1954). *(From her autobiography,* India Calling, *1934)*

5. Edith Smith, depicted in a photo held at Grantham Museum. *(Wikimedia Creative Commons)*

6. The Old Nick Theatre in Gainsborough, Lincolnshire – the old magistrates' court and police station and now a museum and learning centre. The listed building dates back to 1860 and was used by Lincolnshire Constabulary until the 1970s. It was left to the Gainsborough Theatre Company by its businessman owner when he died in 1993. *(Stephen Wade)*

7. London Police Court mission staff. Note the absence of any female workers. *(London Police Court Mission Annual Report for 1893)*

8. Freddy Bywaters, Edith Thompson and the victim, Percy Thompson, July 1921. *(Courtesy of Associated Newspapers Press)*

9. Female convicts at work during the silent hour at Brixton Prison, showing the long supervision required of wardresses when inmates were at work on the wings. *(Mayhew and Binny,* The Criminal Prisons of London, *1862)*

"Lions in Their Dens."

V.—THE LORD LIEUTENANT AT DUBLIN CASTLE.

BY RAYMOND BLATHWAYT.

(Photographs and Illustrations by Lafayette, of Dublin, and Byrne, of Richmond.)

THE HON. MRS ARTHUR HENNIKER.

THE Lord Lieutenant's sister, Mrs. Arthur Henniker, who is helping him to do the honours of the Castle, and whom I had known in London, Mr. Fulke Greville, and I, were wandering round the curious old-fashioned buildings and court-yards that constitute the domain of Dublin Castle one bright breezy day in early spring. A military band was playing opposite the principal entrance, whilst the guard was being mounted in precisely the same manner as at the guard mounting at St. James's. The scene was brilliant and inspiriting in the extreme. As we passed through an archway we came somewhat suddenly upon the massive Round Tower, from the top of which floated the Union Jack, and which dates back to a period not later than that of King John. Close to the Round Tower, which bears so curious a resemblance to the still more magnificent tower of the same name at Windsor, is the Chapel Royal. Here we found the guardian, a quaint, and garrulous and most obliging old person, waiting to show us over the handsome, albeit somewhat gloomy, building. Very exact and particular was our *cicerone* in pointing out to us the old fourteenth century painted windows, the special pews reserved for His Excellency, and the ladies and gentlemen of the court; the coats of arms belonging to the various Governors of Ireland.

10. The wife of the governor at Dublin Castle in the 1890s. A rare glimpse of the supporting and unofficial staff! *(*The Idler, *1893)*

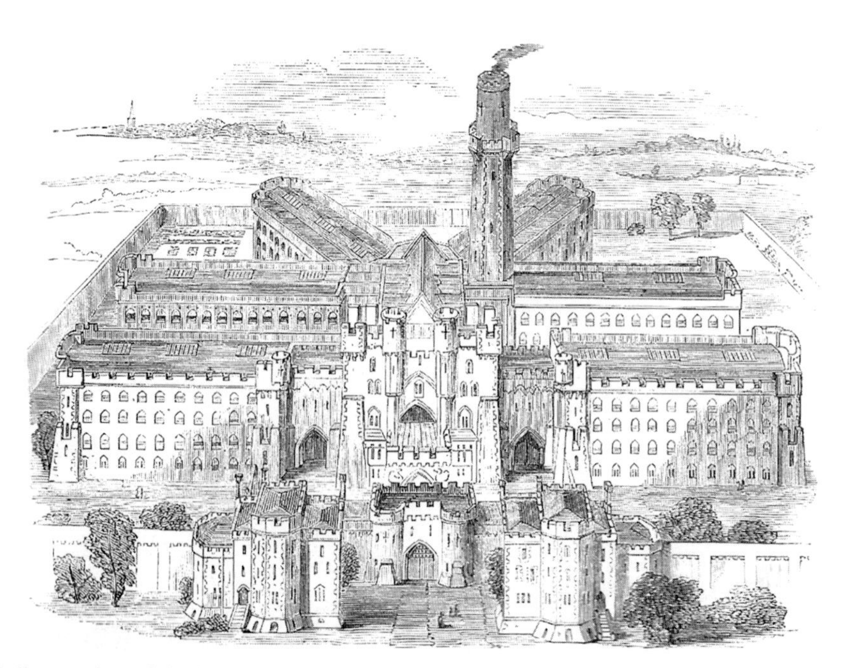

11. Bird's-eye view of the House of Correction for the City of London, Holloway. *(Mayhew and Binny,* The Criminal Prisons of London, *1862)*

12. A rare picture of prison staff in the Victorian period: Northallerton, 1891. The bearded governor in the centre is a survivor of the Charge of the Light Brigade. *(Courtesy of Ripon Police Museum)*

13. Elizabeth Fry (1780-1845) seated at a table surrounded by men and women prisoners listening to her. *(Wikimedia Creative Commons)*

14. The principal matron at the female convict prison, Brixton, c1850. *(Mayhew and Binny,* The Criminal Prisons of London, *1862)*

15. A female inmate of Holloway Prison, c1860, totally anonymous in appearance. *(Mayhew and Binny,* The Criminal Prisons of London, *1862)*

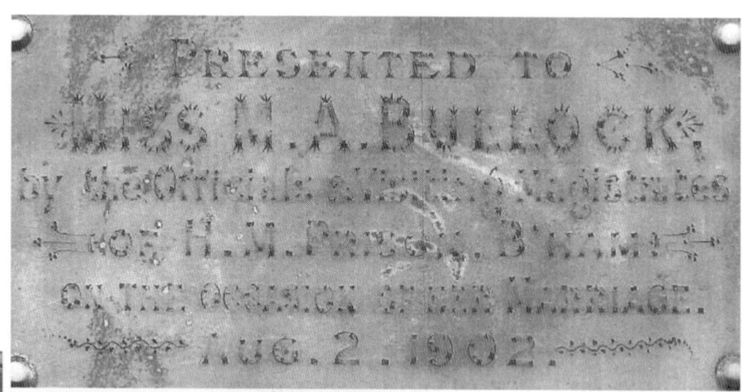

16. The plaque on the chest of drawers presented by the governor and magistrates to Wardress M.A. Bullock of Winson Green Prison, Birmingham, when she married in 1902. *(Courtesy of Ruth Saunders)*

17. Mary Ann Bullock pictured with her daughter Marjorie, c1912. Her attire looks like a prison uniform, with the distinctive full-length skirt, and shirt and collar. *(Courtesy of Ruth Saunders)*

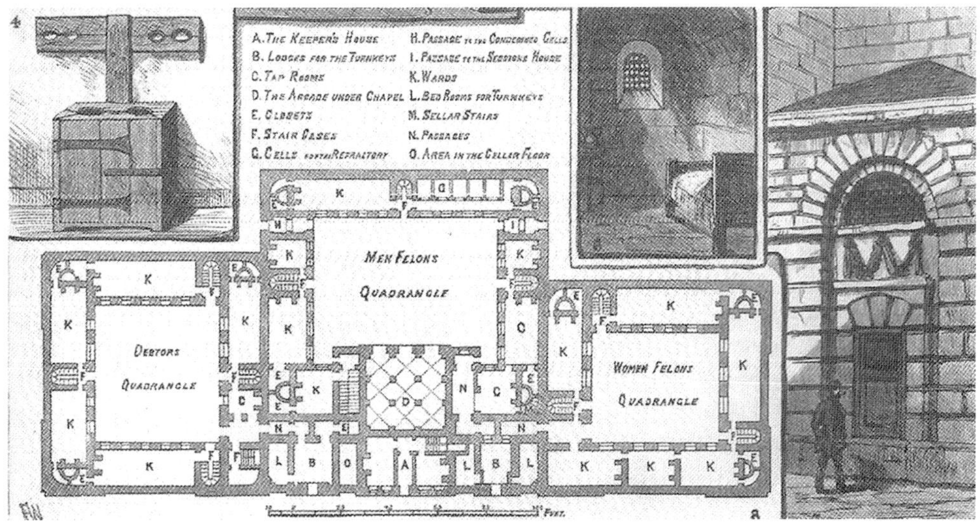

18. A plan of Newgate Prison, c1860. Note the small area allotted to staff – the 'lodge' area. *(Mayhew and Binny,* The Criminal Prisons of London, *1862)*

19. The sign for the WPC Collator Room at Halifax. Women officers worked on administration and intelligence information here up until the 1970s. *(Courtesy of Ripon Police Museum)*

20. A woman police officer enjoys her job, c1930s! *(Courtesy of Metropolitan Police Women's Association)*

21. The women's room at the former Gainsborough Police Station, c1940s. *(Courtesy of the Old Nick Theatre)*

22. A WPC in plain clothes as part of a reconstruction in the Walter Rowland murder case, 1946. *(Author's collection)*

23. Sir William Searle Holdsworth (1871-1944), sitting for the camera, proudly wearing the distinctive judge's wig. *(Wikimedia Creative Commons)*

24. An obvious satire on women's professional aspirations. *(Author's collection)*

had no identity, and the wardresses' roles were to maintain that sense of nameless, time-stopped non-being that a Victorian prison created in its denizens. (See plates 15 and 18)

Today, Holloway is the largest British prison dealing with women prisoners. At the time of the suffragette imprisonment, when women prisoners were force-fed and brutally treated, the inmates gave us some views of the wardresses, and such details are rare. For instance, Constance Lytton, in Holloway, wrote that 'They were fine looking women, young and vigorous, most of them had good figures and all of them had beautifully kept hair which gave me a deal of pleasure to look at.... They held themselves very upright, and their general bearing brought to my mind certain types on the chaperon's bench at Court balls.'

When Constance was force-fed, in Walton Prison, Liverpool, after the ordeal, back in her cell, she wrote: 'The wardresses were kind and knelt round to comfort me, but there was nothing to be done.' And again, 'The wardress who came most often to my cell was kind to me.' Certainly, the evidence points to wardresses being generally far from the image we might think of from the media – that of severe, rather cruel disciplinarians. In the case of the suffragettes and force-feeding, they had unpleasant tasks to do, holding down the women while the doctor fed a tube into the gullet, and everything had to be done according to rules, but they seem to have had a high degree of understanding and warmth when needed.

Our insights into the nature of the wardresses are from fragmentary parts of documentary projects or from brief memoirs and comments included in enquiries or in biography. Such material is in the writings of another suffragette, Susan Willis Fletcher, who was in prison long before the early twentieth-century agitations, being in Tothill Fields Prison in the 1870s. She gives an account of an aspect of the wardresses that might easily be overlooked: the role that some of them took as real friends (something that is anathema in prison work today). Fletcher quotes a letter she received on release from this wardress, which includes these words: 'I am passing that old cell. I look in. It is empty – no one there.

Then I don't know what to do with myself. Oh do forgive me. I ought not to remind you of this dreadful place, but I do miss you so much.'

In the early years of the nineteenth century, the French writer and socialist Flora Tristan (as noted in my first chapter) visited prisons in London, and one of her experiences in meeting a wardress once again backs up the sense we have of their caring and concern. In Newgate, a woman prisoner caught Flora's eye as being notably dignified and controlled. Her story was that she had sold rented furniture in order to stave off hunger in her young family. She had been abandoned by her sailor husband and was in extreme distress when she committed the crime. Flora's account of the wardress is a rare insight: 'Oh madame … this poor young woman deserves your pity … she was driven out of her mind by poverty … she has been here for two months awaiting trial.' Flora adds that the wardress spoke 'in a low voice because she did not want other prisoners to hear, and because she did not want her words to hurt the feelings of the young mother'.

There is no doubt that the work of a prison warder (or 'officer', as they came to be called by the post-war years) entails at times a kind of relationship that has some aspects of what would ordinarily be called a friendship: there is so much emotional dimension to the prisoner's situation, of course. But professionals doing prison work know, and have always known, that the relationship is strictly in line with the minutiae in the job description.

This was highlighted in the most militant years of the suffragette demonstrations and campaigns as well, notably in the wardresses' behaviour during the barbaric force-feeding episodes. In Katherine Willoughby Marshall's memoirs, for instance, she writes: 'The wardresses, as a whole, were quite as kind as one would expect, and later on, when they knew they could trust the suffragettes, they let us have our doors open a little for half an hour on a Sunday afternoon. We had no windows that opened and only a stuffy ventilator, so quite a number of girls had to go to hospital because of their health.'

A more typical record of a woman officer's behaviour is seen in the biography of Nell Duncan, who was in Holloway Prison in the 1940s. Her biographer wrote:

> On visitor's day, Nell swung a shoddy vampire-style cloak over her prison uniform, and followed a prison guard.
>
> 'Over there. Take a seat at the table,' the wardress ordered.... The door at the end of the room opened wide and Jean walked towards Nell.... Nell swallowed Jean up in a grateful hug. The wardress stepped forward. 'That's quite enough contact,' she ordered.

By the mid-twentieth century, and indeed up to the 1970s, there were mounting problems for female wardresses, and these, research has shown, were partly because of prejudice and denigration. One researcher, as recently as 2000, described the situation here with regard to the integration (or lack of it) of women officers on the wings: 'Although women officers are welcomed into the service at the recruitment stage, some find that once on the landings of male prisons, they are not fully accepted by their male colleagues.'

Then there is the issue of leadership and management: what about women governors? Attention was first given to the office of governor as early as 1839 in the Act for the Better Ordering of Prisons. The definition given there is simple: the magistrates 'shall appoint such keeper by the style of governor. Such governor shall have all the powers and duties of the gaoler or keeper of that prison.' David Wilson, himself a governor in recent times, explains the early thinking on the matter: 'The title governor was associated with the rise in social standing of the occupation; many authorities introduced the term in an attempt to improve the dignity of the office. Governor was evocative of deputising duties on behalf of a higher authority; an image reminiscent of colonial administration.'

In 1922, Fenner Brockway made an important point about the office: 'No particular qualifications are demanded by law, and the frequency with which retired military and naval officers are appointed indicates that disciplinary capacity is primarily considered … of the twenty-six prison governors, twenty-four have served with the regular forces.' Hence the absence of women governors until the 1970s, when the main aspect of the job was seen as management. By 1972, the job description entailed 'a knowledge of specialist skills and resources available for their [the prisoners'] treatment and rehabilitation'.

After the Second World War, British prisons were beset by all kinds of problems, from overcrowding, to an intolerable frequency of escapes. The papers were repeatedly carrying features on this parlous state of affairs, but they also relished the notion of a documentary approach as well, and as the first women governors were coming into the system by that time, reporters were attracted to rather cheery, novelty pieces on the women who ruled behind bars. A typical example is a feature from 1964 on HMP Styal, near Manchester.

The anonymous correspondent noted that the governor called out good morning to some prisoners: 'The ladies were some of the 175 involuntary residents of the new Styal prison for women which, at the end of its first year of existence is justifying all the hope placed in it.' The governor in question was Miss McWilliam, and the writer makes it clear that the regime is one concerned with innovation and improvement: 'Her dossier of the signs of success is beginning to build up – snapshots of happy families at the seaside, letters describing the redecorating of the kitchen and asking for advice on wallpaper.' The reporter did, however, ask about the key question of what the prison achieves, and the conclusion was: 'The deprivation of liberty is still the greatest deterrent that remains,' said McWilliam, who also gave her opinion on something more fundamental: 'Like most women prison officers, she believes that the intrinsically evil woman is a very rare creature indeed and that when members of her sex get into trouble it is usually because of circumstances.'

By the 1980s there was a reorganization of governor grades, from one to five, and the figures for 1997 reflect a quiet revolution – the emergence of women governors. At that date there were forty-two grade one governors, of whom two were women. In the overall figure of 475 people of governor grades, fifty-five were women. By the early twenty-first century, women governors were a familiar sight across the prison estate. Some idea of the massive changes that have taken place in the management of prisons may be gained by noting that, for example, in 2002 one of the most challenging gaols, Belmarsh, had a woman governor (Hazel Banks); the top security prison Full Sutton had a woman as education manager and a woman in the role of chair of the Board of Visitors. In Styal, a women's prison, in that same year, both governors, the head of healthcare and the senior probation officer were women.

Even as recently as the 1950s, matters were still little different for wardresses. In the Prison Act of that year, for instance, in clauses relating to prison officers, we have this:

> Where any living accommodation is provided for a prison officer and his family by virtue of his office, then, if he ceases to be a prison officer or is suspended from office or dies, he, or as the case may be, his family, shall quit the accommodation when required to do so by notice of the Secretary of State.

Little had changed since Brockway's reports of 1922.

More recent studies have highlighted the issues of women officers working in a traditionally male environment, and in most cases, the conclusions drawn have to relate to the category and nature of the prison in question. There is a vast difference between a borstal, for instance, and a local prison; immense differences exist when we compare a category A (top security) prison such as Full Sutton in Yorkshire, with a category D (open) prison such as North Sea Camp. But studies of female officers in prison work have brought to light many of the elements of the work that would have been left unspoken for several decades before the massive changes in the philosophy and management of prisons that took place in the 1990s.

An example of this is a feature written by Neelama Kumari and others, and published in 2012. These writers studied the therapeutic community of Grendon Prison, beginning their report with the bold statement that 'Traditionally, prisons are male dominated places.' They set out to look at the experiences of women working in such an environment. Their conclusions were that all was not perfect in terms of gender roles, but that the regime was safe and that prisoners showed respect to staff. The shadow over this is surely in this statement: 'There are still predominantly males in senior roles ... but participants did report feeling that their achievements are recognized at Grendon.'

Further writing on the subject has been more energetically encouraged and produced in recent years, including a detailed survey of the prison officer generally in a work edited by Alison Liebling, *The Prison Officer* (2011), in which she and her fellow authors look into many of the common complaints about women working in these jobs. One conclusion they quote from previous work is notably important: 'The main differences found between male and female officers is that there is a lower incidence of marriage and dependent children among female officers and a higher level of education. Male officers are more likely to have a trade or technical qualification.' This is surely one of the causes of a noted increase in the proportion of women working in governor grades after the administration of prisons was revised and reordered in the 1990s.

In the last twenty years, as the number of female officers has gradually increased, what has happened is significant in a number of ways. Many of the fears expressed regarding the safety of females in the job, and about their tendency to be 'softer' on inmates, would seem to be unfounded. Women officers have had to learn to counter these opinions by aligning attitudes and behaviour with the male stance taken on relationships with prisoners. But equally, it may be argued that women's more sophisticated emotional literacy has given them an advantage and in fact made them influential in the process of change among some of the male staff.

The conclusion must be, after a wide-ranging survey of how and why there has been a steadily increasing number of women officers working in the prison estate, that there are primarily aspects of the work relating to the essential building of trust and caring as well as the discipline that are integral to the occupation. The thinking behind the female presence in prison work mostly relates to the need to minimize confrontational situations, and to work on professional relationships within the walls that function daily on an attainable basis of mutual respect and consideration. Too often in the past, as we know from prison memoirs, the 'macho culture' of the offenders and the 'canteen culture' of the male officers have maintained a divisive foundation in the regime. Prison has to work, in spite of all its inherent problems and stresses, on a certain balance between empathic thinking by the staff and on a more objective view being taken by the prisoners.

There is little doubt that today the 'macho culture' has been tempered to some degree by the increase in female staff. Common sense dictates that, faced with a woman making a request of a prisoner on a landing of a wing or in a cell, there is much less sense of a confrontation, a clash of egos and self-respect. Negotiation and fair dealing play a large part in all such transactions, and everything has to be built on trust. It may well be – and research has yet to show this convincingly – that the female presence in the body of prison staff actually helps things run more smoothly because of women's wider span of language use and appreciation of the nuances involved in speaking of emotions and family relationships.

Chapter 6

Wartime and Post-war Policewomen

We didn't do trauma.
Interview with Sandra Wilkinson, police officer in the 1960s

During the war, the organization known as Mass Observation, a nationwide documentary project that aimed to use volunteer diary keepers to register social life and work, asked interviewees the question, 'Should married women be able to go out to work after the war?' The answers give some clues as to the change in attitudes, now that two world wars had proved that women could do a range of professional work more than capably. But they also remind the reader that the topic is fraught with difficulties, naturally based on the work/home/children interplay. For instance, some women looked at the topic with a sense of a real overview: 'The proportion of women with a real flair for business or talents for the professions or arts, to the ordinary ones, is very small.'

In contrast, other women saw the need for state help in order to achieve equality of opportunity: 'If they want to, I see no reason why they should not, and I think there should be a state scheme to enable them to have time off to have children.' Perhaps the norm is expressed in this reply: 'Very maternal women would obviously stay with their young children. The other sort would send them to nursery schools where they would be much happier … many women who love their children dearly are yet incapable of coping with them all day and every day.'

It is clear from newspapers, periodicals, surveys and autobiographies of the time, that in terms of such professions as those in the law and administration, higher education and politics, the war and its aftermath created a number of openings for 'career women' and in the police in particular, there was a slow realization that women staff in all contexts had a great deal to offer. (See plate 20)

However, during the war, old habits of thought died hard. Writing about the criminal justice system often highlighted the entrenched attitudes, sometimes seen more in selection of information, and omission, so that readers today gather details of attitudes by what is not said rather than what is said.

For instance, in 1940, Sir Maurice Amos was given the task of writing a succinct account of the British justice system. He managed to produce a booklet of fifty-two pages, covering every aspect of importance. When it came to surveying the nature of the police forces, he felt that mention should be made of the women police. They were worth a paragraph:

> An interesting and important development of recent years has been in the enrolment of women police, who have proved particularly useful in the performance of duties relating to women and children. In June, 1938, there were sixty-eight policewomen in London, and 111 in the boroughs and counties. Gloucestershire recently had four policewomen who covered rural areas on motorcycles.

There are several interesting implications to this brief account. First, Amos has confirmed the limited area of work the women police supposedly experience; second, he picks out a provincial development as a curiosity. In his booklet, the special constables were given four times the space. However, in spite of these restricted views of what was becoming increasingly important, the war proved the women officers' usefulness. Amos's attitude reflects the pervading point of view on the subject: although women had proved their worth in all kinds of traditionally male jobs in the Great War, surely, the thinking went, in normal circumstances, they don't really wear uniforms and carry any authority, do they? The challenge for the women in blue was to wear down such attitudes.

Throughout the war years and after, one of the central issues for the police was the development of a women's police constabulary. In

1940 a circular was sent out to police authorities promoting the idea of recruiting women police. At the end of 1939 there were just 230 women constables in England; the railway police had appointed their first women in the 1930s and the time was ripe, given wartime extreme conditions, to start work on achieving a more widespread policewoman constabulary. The first aim was for a women's auxiliary police corps. In Birmingham, the chief constable had already agreed to set up a training course for women; their duties were primarily seen as in traffic control, driving, maintenance of police equipment and canteen work. Through modern eyes, that seems ridiculously condescending and was, of course, in line with dominant ideologies of gender at the time. No doubt male officers thought all of that quite right and fitting for the 'fairer sex' and also some thought that policing was men's work and should stay that way.

But in 1940, a writer to *The Times* pointed out that women police were needed then more than ever. The reason was that 'The help and guidance of women police would do much towards the safety of our young men and women, and their steadying presence would be a valuable factor in case of panic.' The writer also pointed out that police authorities had not responded to the Home Secretary's appeal and found it disgusting that 'such blindness and inertia' should be tolerated. By February 1941, there was a more forthright appeal for recruits. London needed women police; they were to be 'unmarried, or widows of under thirty-five, of good character and keenness and of good physique'. They were required to be over 5 feet 4 inches tall and the pay was to be £3 2s 6d a week. There had been a case in which women officers had been notably effective: 'Two of them in particular displayed exceptional abilities at a time when London was being troubled by the outbreak of violence by members of the illegal Irish Republican Army.'

There was still a shortage of women officers in 1944. The Archbishop of Canterbury, Dr Temple, also joined in the appeal, saying at a massive conference of women's organizations: 'For instance, there was the help which women police could give to women and children who might be destitute and to those who might be victims of sexual offences.... Some policemen could do this, but they were very few.' This was certainly backed up by other commentators, such as John Watson of the Southwark Juvenile Court, who had written about 'street corner boys and girls' and he pointed out that they often stood in his courtroom 'as the culmination of a series of unhappy adventures in which sex played a leading part'.

A significant event – but one that was hardly marked with any real celebration or media promotion – was the appointment of the first female chief inspector at Scotland Yard in December 1945. This was Group Officer E.C. Bather of the WAAF. There was already a superintendent of women police, Miss D. Peto, but her career also had been unnoticed by the press.

In the City of London Police, finally, the initiative was confidently followed. In 1949, the proposition was made for a City force of women police. The City commissioner wanted to employ one woman sergeant and six women constables, bringing the number of City police personnel to 982. As always when it came to City initiatives, the press liked to point out the cost. In this case that would be an increase of just over £3,000 in the first year. Why similar figures were rarely given for Metropolitan projects is not clear.

There were many significant developments in the story of women police from the 1950s onwards, as noted in the timeline of the British Association of Women Policing. For instance, in 1950 the first women sergeants were appointed in the British Transport Police; from 1963 there were training conferences organized by the International Association of Women Police; and in 1969, in less enlightened times, there was great media interest in the appointment of the Metropolitan Police's first black female officer, Sislin Allen. In 1967 there were more than 3,000 women police officers in England and Wales, and thirty years later, 22 per cent of police applicants were female.

The 1975 Sex Discrimination Act meant the end of segregated lifestyles for male and female officers. Previously, in local stations, women had been given their own rooms and facilities, and indeed they had their own rank structure, along with demarcated tasks in their job profile. (See plates 19 and 21)

One of the best ways to tell the story of women police and their experience in the years between the end of the war and c1970, when radical changes occurred, is to look at officers' memoirs.

Sandra Wilkinson, for instance, worked as a police officer in the 1960s, in the regions, not in London. Before that service, she had worked as a secretary, working in the backroom, as it were, supporting police investigations, and one of these was in what has become known as the Moors Murders. The following is an account of my interview with her.

Sandra has a good stock of scrapbooks about her involvement in one of the major murder enquiries in the history of crime. As we looked through them and she pointed out locations on Saddleworth Moor, or talked about a woman detective she knew, I felt as if I was revisiting a dark place in history. She showed me her photograph, as in the *Daily Mirror* at the time when Brady and Hindley were tried at Chester Assizes. Here was a woman with a story to tell, and it had been a long time since she showed these cuttings to anyone.

We met by chance. I write about true crime and spend hours in libraries and archives. Most of this work is about old newsprint and fading photos you find on a blurry microfilm image. But here was that rare thing, a chance to talk about a period in modern history when police work was just emerging from its *Blue Lamp* image and was being given to us as something close to the 'new documentary'. Not that it was being glamorized in the writing of the 1960s. Quiet heroism and career problems seemed to be the order of the day, and a PC was very non-PC by today's standards.

Sandra stepped into this world of mean streets and macho talk, and her photos show her wearing the stylish dark cape designed by no less a fashion guru than Norman Hartnell. But the impression she gives is that it wasn't macho at all – more gentlemanly. After all, this is the time in which it was considered unacceptable to swear on the football terraces if a woman was present. At the time, she was just taking up duties in Birkenhead. Her days as a secretary to the team of detectives who combed the wilds of Saddleworth were behind her. The Sandra of these images is every inch the professional, standing by a Panda car, or looking firm and controlled outside a police station. She displays the virtues of the British police as I recall them, in my teenage life in Leeds in the sixties: strong, visible, reliable, demanding respect.

The training course for this new life was at Padgate, Warrington. Sandra remembers this with real affection. 'It was the best time of my life … I wept buckets when we had to leave,' she says. She knows the date as soon as she is asked: 6 October 1968. It was a year of riot and unrest over the Channel, and here we were losing several layers of innocence about modernity as well. You might say that at this point, our conceptions of the police were changing radically, as was the case with the entire notion of authority.

She notes that there was much pride in the training. There may have been a lively social side to the time, with entertainment being produced as part of the deal, but it was also tough. The drilling square was in use by eight in the morning and then it was down to some hard studying. All the details are still there as she fills in the picture. The famous cape was excellent quality, and the Cheshire force had a much better standard of dress than the Manchester outfit. Sandra tells me that some of the badges were enamelled. All the official photos show a woman completely comfortable in her position, status and very obvious responsibility. The car shines, well cared for. The hat and jacket are immaculate.

From the seminar room and the role plays it was out into the stuff of life. Her photographs reflect that quasi-military life and the facial expressions are firm, in control. Yes, she had experienced a certain notoriety during the previous few years, as fate brought her a central role in a media show as the tabloids struggled to find ways of extracting daily stories from Hyde while the force was out combing the moors. But nothing in that phase prepared Sandra for the police work on the streets. She had been only nineteen when she began work as secretary for Bob Talbot and the Moors team.

But in police work, she witnessed things that affected her deeply, such as being there when a mother callously rejected her own child, telling her to her face that she wanted nothing to do with her. 'That was the worst thing I ever saw,' she says. But when I ask about the traumatic experiences in a police career, she smiles and says, 'We didn't do trauma … there was no time.'

Whereas in the Moors investigation she had sat in the incident room and answered the phone, now in uniform, she saw pain and suffering at first hand. She brings to mind one quiet Sunday morning and the harrowing experience of seeing the charred bodies of six children in the back of a car after a man had shot through some lights at high speed, just shattering the peace of that weekend lull in between the Saturday drunks and the afternoon in the park.

Of course, I have to mention the image of the macho, unreformed male in the police, slotted into our consciousness through a thousand television dramas since *Z Cars*. But Sandra is eager to put me right on this one. She uses the word camaraderie, and explains that there was professional respect, and that teamwork was at the core of everything. She talks about 'gentlemanly' officers and a very different basis of relationships in the force, reflecting a world with just as many social problems as now, but maybe more easily understood and remedied.

As for her work in the Moors case, it is a fascinating chapter of history in the annals of modern police work. It was a steady, regular and ordered enquiry, with meticulous monitoring and recording. I picture her alone in the central office as the world's press darted around frantically outside. In a pre-computer age, the office work functioned around phone calls, record cards and a coded range of knocks on the office wall: one for tea, two for a useful communication and three for 'get out there now!'

The days of the enquiry were long and hard, Sandra being collected at 8.30 in the morning, taken to the office in Hyde, and then work progressing steadily right through to eight at night.

The journalists and writers flocked to Hyde and to Sandra's office. She met Emlyn Williams, the author of the first book on the case, *Beyond Belief*. She and a friend were dogged by reporters and they sometimes had to hide. The whole business became so farcical that one day a newspaperman came into her office pretending to be ill. His performance was worthy of Olivier, but transparently sham. She had to fuss and seem concerned, while all the time watching him like a hawk.

The team managed to snatch an hour at the Queen's Head in Hyde for some bonding, but Sandra stresses that the talk on these occasions was strictly unwinding, easy small talk. There is nothing sensational in her memories of the time. It was 'just careful, routine work, as with any case … we had no idea at the time that this was to be momentous, and in so many books.'

She always wanted to be a police officer, from the time of her first job as a clerk in a magistrate's court, but never dreamed that a few years on from that, she would be snapped by the *Mirror* cameraman. I sense that, even today, when her early career and the story of those awful child murders is 'classic crime' history, there is a certain respectful reserve in her attitude, and every sentence she utters has a tone of a less hectic and more people-centred time. I can imagine her on the beat or taking a call, and I feel assured that she would have been totally professional. Her most frequent word when talking about colleagues from that time is 'gentleman'.

After the interview, I understand why she chooses to say more about policing Birkenhead than what Myra Hindley said to her in the office. It has something to do with actually doing something positive to help out on the streets and in the unhappy homes. The psychopaths can be left to specialists and therapists, but there are plain folk out there being robbed and attacked or just drinking too much and disturbing the peace … and you can do something about that.

As she sat in that office, at times there had been Ian Brady in the room behind her. Now he is an old man in jail and he has known no other life for decades.

For a London perspective on the work of women police officers, Joan Lock's account in her book *Lady Policeman* (1968) offers a rounded account of the duties and the range of experience the work entailed. Her time on the beat included posing as a prostitute, checking out waifs and strays, missing persons, petty theft, drunk people, aliens and other random street problems from insane characters to pimps.

Joan is candid and entertaining when writing about her police experience. She writes that 'The mainstay of women police work in the West End was "stops in the street". The Metropolitan Police use two Acts of Parliament which give them this power. The Metropolitan Police Act gives the right to stop, search and detain a person reasonably suspected of having stolen property, whilst the Children and Young Persons Act allows the stopping of suspected absconders.'

She then recounts a range of cases in which she and fellow officers were in pursuit of young people who had run away from home or from some kind of approved school. The work, as Joan makes clear, entailed being as clever and streetwise as the girls on the run, and the accounts of how identity was ascertained in these cases give a rare insight into the kind of police work that women did at the time.

Joan was in service at the time when the old attitudes of having women officers for a circumscribed range of duties, fitting for a woman, were still dominant. One instance she gives of this is in a job at a Mayfair club. She recalls that she was told, 'Go to this ladies' club in Mayfair and sit with one of the employees until the DAO arrives.… There's a POC there already and he'll hang on if necessary.' What followed was that a women washer-up was walking around, dressed in nothing but a vest, after having refused to go and enjoy her holiday time, on pay. The women was dressed, and then undressed herself completely. She was agitated and was trying hard to get back to her work. Then, being restrained, 'She urinated on the floor.' She had a stash of banknotes that she had saved, and Joan writes, 'Some of the notes were getting soaked but she became more upset when we tried to rescue them.' Eventually, Joan had to gather all the money and count it, and the lady was taken to hospital. Joan notes, 'I went to wash the urine from my hands.'

Joan describes something that is crucially important to the lives of women police at this time: the training received. While men trained at the Police College at Hendon in the 1960s, women went to Peel House at Victoria.

There was, at the very beginning of course, distribution and supply of uniforms and basic drill. Then came the substance of the course: 'three months of hard mental graft with oceans of stuff to be learned parrot-fashion.' In addition, there were role-plays, mock incidents and first aid.

We also learn from Joan Lock something about the recruits: 'The women police were a mixed lot but in the main consisted of ex-secretaries, bank clerks, teachers and nurses.' Naturally, as the women were to work primarily on family cases and relationships disputes, they had special courses covering those subjects. As Joan reflects, there were also a surprisingly high number of incest cases. Her conclusions are that the course was sometimes interesting and sometimes boring, but the curriculum was certainly wide: as well as visits to places of relevance to police work, there were a number of specialists who came to give lectures, such as psychiatrists and children's officers. Of course, they had a taste of prison life, at Holloway, and although they were in plain clothes, Joan notes that they were known, as she had a comment: 'Here's some of the girls from West End Central.'

By the 1970s, with massive social changes, together with shifts in the patterns and nature of crime, there were reassessments of the structure of the police. One important element in this was recruitment, which had to change with the changing times. Back in the early days of the 'Peelers' the stress had been placed on signing up farm workers as police constables: big, sturdily built men who could look intimidating and use muscle when required.

In 1967, when the Home Office commissioned a report on the recruitment of people with higher education qualifications, the police establishment was catching up with the new professionalism of other organizations. Education was open to working-class people then, and it was high time that police staff had more graduates among them. At the opening of the report, the authors stated:

> Pay scales are different for men and women, and no woman has been appointed chief constable or assistant chief constable, although there

> are two Assistant Inspectors of Constabulary. But women police officers are eligible for, and attend, courses at the Police College, and the rules governing promotion are the same for men as for women. We believe that the police service offers a stimulating and rewarding career to well educated women, and the recommendations that follow … apply equally to men.

Clearly, the authors could not see and understand that their first statement on equal pay would be a major deterrent to those new women graduates who otherwise might have chosen the police as a career, as opposed to being solicitors, teachers or social workers. There is a worrying element of the 'token woman' in the report, as if the authors felt they had to add a statement to make them appear liberal and forward thinking.

There has always been one particularly interesting and important role played by women police officers – literally 'acting' a part – and that is being involved in re-enactments of crimes. A typical example of this in the early days of such cases was concerned in a Leeds murder that remains unsolved to this day.

Mary Judge was well known around the area of Leeds along Kirkgate, between the Parish Church and the Regent Hotel. It is a few streets of dark alleys, not far from the Calls – notoriously unsafe places for walks by night forty years ago. But Mary, forty years old and a cheery, sociable person, liked a drink and liked that area: in many ways a risky business, as may be seen even today, because there is a patch of land (now a small park and well maintained) under the railway arches. The trains above tend to swing around on the viaduct before going on into the station a short way further into the centre of the city.

Mary was discovered by a passer-by just before midnight on 22 February 1968, battered and mostly naked, with her clothes scattered around her body. She was only 5 feet 5, with brown hair, and had been wearing quite garish clothes, definitely not colour co-ordinated, so that would have made her noticeable. Her skirt was dark blue, the shoes green, white blouse, and her coat was a black check. She had severe head injuries.

The area was sealed off and arc lights set up in that dismal, shadowy patch of land. Superintendent Hoban of Leeds CID had barriers erected and asked about Mary's life. She was well known to the barmen of the pubs around there, such as the Brougham, the Regent and other places up Kirkgate. People said she was 'always friendly and happy, liked a drink, and loved to stop and talk to children'. The patch of land is close to the Leeds City Bus Station, and at that time the area was notorious for its attraction to beggars and tramps. Tramps would often cadge money along the bus station platforms. By day it was busy: there was a huge Pilkington's Glass office nearby, and commuter crowds would walk from the buses, past the abattoir to Vicar Lane. By night, it has to be said, the area was well frequented by prostitutes too. Whether Mary was on the game is not clear, but one interesting point is that she lived in East End Park, on Glendale Street. This was a long walk for her, up towards the Shaftesbury cinema along the York Road. If she was a familiar figure down by the buses, she needed a good reason to walk more than a mile down to the pubs she liked – and alone.

But Mary's murder has a fascinating piece of drama to it: people saw her being attacked. This was because the Hull train rattled past the Parish Church at 10.18 that night, and several people saw the assailant. A small boy was the main witness. He came forward with his mother and gave a description of a tall man of slim build, with long dark hair and wearing a dark suit. Of course, this was February in Yorkshire; but the train passed within a mere 50 yards of the patch of grass where the killing happened. The 8.37 train from Hull would prove to be a key element in the investigation into the heartless slaughter.

Mary had also been seen outside the Regent Hotel in Kirkgate earlier that night, and it also became obvious that the killer would have had plenty of her blood on his clothes. Appeals were made to local dry cleaners to be vigilant in inspecting clothes brought in for cleaning in the day after the killing. Nothing came of that, so the train sightings became the main leads.

The Hull train was so important that a reconstruction was staged. Officers boarded a train at Cross Gates, and PC Eileen Playforth took the part of poor Mary Judge. It took just fifteen seconds for the train to pass the scene; it was winter, late at night, and the grass was under the tall arches of the high viaduct. But one positive thing emerged from this: a man was seen leaving the scene by a Bradford man, another passenger on that Hull train. At that point on the train's journey, and passing quite high over the patch of grass, the view would be quite distorted. But there was enough seen to make a helpful descriptive statement.

Yet all this work and methodical investigation brought no positive result. Mary, a friendly woman who may have simply been lonely, and not looking for men-friends at all, was brutally killed. But whether she was in the area for financial reasons or simply to meet friends, there was a certain degree of risk in that place at that time.

Of course, readers of true crime stories like an unsolved crime: it opens up the possibility that the reader might come up with a theory. The Judge case is for sure a 'cold case' now but everyone lives in hope of something turning up. After all, a murder that took place in Halifax in 1957 (again a woman on her own) was thought to be permanently unsolved until a few years ago when Calderdale Police received a phone call referring to a man's deathbed confession.

WPC Playforth had to 'be' Mary Judge – to move in and out of the places Mary would have been in on that fateful night. As we read the account of the case today, it is easy to overlook the highly demanding part Constable Playforth had to play, making sure she was at the right spot when the Hull train went across the viaduct.

No account of women police since the 1940s would be complete without some account of the women who have made the ultimate sacrifice in the course of their work. The advent of terrorism enters the story here. In 1983, outside Harrods, a week before Christmas, the Provisional IRA left an Austin 130 GT parked in Hans Crescent. By lunchtime that day, a phone call was made to the Samaritans, giving details of the car bomb in the Austin.

The area was soon being searched by officers in Knightsbridge, and the car was spotted, parked near to Harrods. Although the area around the parked car was demarcated and marked by cones, some police arrived by car and stopped close by. Three personnel in the car got out and walked towards the Austin: Inspector Dodd, Sergeant Lane and WPC Jane Arbuthnot. As they walked, the bomb went off. Only Inspector Dodd survived the scene, but he too died on Christmas Eve. The officers were not the only casualties: in all, seventy-eight people were injured and two members of the public also died.

WPC Arbuthnot had only been in the police for just over two years.

Surely the most well-known police death in the ranks of women officers killed is Yvonne Fletcher, who had wanted to be in the police since she was a little girl; she was destined to die on a day that began like any other day on police duty. On 17 April 1984, she was part of a large detachment with the job of supervising a demonstration of Libyans in St James's Square, where they were shouting against the Gaddafi regime.

The situation escalated into something more large scale when some Gaddafi supporters arrived and set up against the first arrivals, across the square. Yvonne Fletcher was standing close to the anti-Gaddafi crowd when a man came out from a room on the first floor of the Libyan People's Bureau and shot her in the back. Officers went to help her and she was rushed to Westminster Hospital, but there she died shortly after arrival.

Those deaths were in relation to major international events and confrontations, but women police officers risk their lives every time they walk out on a beat, along with their male colleagues, of course, and routine work can go wrong, despite the most careful planning. That was the case with the death of WPC Nina Mackay in October 1997, when she went with a Support Group to gain entry to a property where Magdi Elgizouli, a Somalian, was situated, and wanted for a breach of bail conditions. Nina arrived with the team and she had the task of using the 'enforcer' for breaking in the door. Unfortunately, she took off her police armour in order to use the tool effectively, and she could not get out of the way of the charge of her colleagues, being knocked down some stairs, where the wanted man stabbed her with a knife. She died two hours later in hospital. Nina had been in the police for five years.

The police roll of honour for women officers, run by the Police Memorial Trust, lists sixty deaths on duty, the first being Bertha Gleghorn, who was on duty at Tottenham Court Road police station when it was hit by a flying bomb in 1944.

In the last twenty years there has been a remarkable acceleration in the process of change for women police officers, in a variety of contexts. Some events really stand out, however, such as the appointment of Pauline Clare as Chief Constable for Lancashire – the first women to have that high rank. Overall, in the last few decades, there has been a further quiet revolution in the service, as new concepts of police duties and ways of working in a changing society have evolved. One notable landmark was in 2001, when the British Association for Women in Policing created its 'Gender Agenda', which brings together a range of staff representatives from professional bodies within the police forces.

These initiatives have established such fresh and sometimes quite astonishing achievements for women officers that the result has been that we now have women police chiefs regularly dishing out commands and issuing reprimands to their male underlings on such television dramas as *Scott and Bailey* and *Lewis*. Compared with a hundred years ago, when the powerless women police pioneers were not only teased and reviled but prosecuted over trivia, and from the viewpoint of 1914, their future looked bleak, today, women in police uniforms are an everyday sight, and there is nothing surprising about detective sergeants being lectured by women superiors.

The media representations do not shy away from depicting the work done by women police officers as being extremely dangerous; their lives are at risk at any time, as the recent murders of WPCs Nicola Hughes and Fiona Bone in Manchester demonstrated so tragically.

Chapter 7

Probation Officers and Legal Executives

I've got a little list
Of society offenders who might well be underground ...
Gilbert and Sullivan, *The Mikado*

In most chapters, I have touched on the workers who have always been behind the scenes in the criminal justice system. These have included women working in the police court missions, in prisons as 'unofficial staff' being family members, statement takers in the police, and court staff supporting magistrates and barristers. Now the focus is on them so that there is a fuller understanding of the whole picture.

Usually, in researching information about such workers from past sources there are mere glimpses, as in an educational publication of 1970 in which a small photograph is included with the caption 'Picking up an object with a handkerchief often spoils the fingerprints on it. This woman CID officer knows the right way to do it.' It is the only mention of a woman in the whole information pack.

Before we have an account of how women came to work in the probation service, a brief recounting of what existed before probation was established is essential. The story begins with the police court missionaries.

In the course of his work helping criminals in London in the 1890s, Thomas Holmes had some frightening experiences. On one occasion he wrote that he had gone into homes in which wives were shivering with fear and the children ran into safe hiding places as violent men threatened assault. He wrote: 'I have stood in front of these men and have been horribly afraid for my own safety, for with a poker or a hatchet in his hand, a man of this kind needs wary dealing. I know these men are mad but I know that no doctor will certify them as such.'

Holmes was one of the breed of unsung heroes who worked with the London underclass, trying to keep them from prison and a life of crime, years before there were professional probation officers after the 1907 Act. He was born in Walsall in 1846, and he became an iron-moulder, like his father. He worked in this trade until his early thirties, but also spent time teaching the working classes. After a serious accident, he was advised to apply to become a police court missionary. In 1885 he was successful, being attached to Lambeth Police Court. Holmes later wrote two books on his experiences, and in one of these he explains that he actually had a moment of epiphany that led to his new life.

If your ancestor was one of the thousands of poor and deprived Londoners who found themselves on the wrong side of the law in late Victorian Britain, then the chances are that one of the missionaries worked with them and tried to help them.

As the nineteenth century wore on, the volume of petty crime increased so much that the old system of what were called summary courts was increasingly organized and administered by the police rather than by legal professionals of various kinds. A massive influence on this accelerating volume of crime was drunkenness, so it is no accident that the missionaries had their roots in the Temperance movement. The Inebriates Act of 1898 made it possible for the courts to send drunks to a reformatory, and there were a number of homes for inebriates. But back in 1876, when the police court missionaries idea was born, there was nothing to help the women or juveniles on the streets scraping a living through selling anything from trinkets and matches to sex.

The human traffic passing through the police courts reflected the dismal failures of the affluent society of Victorian Britain, with its proud boast of wealth and progress, which was displayed in The Great Exhibition of 1851. Beneath the glamour and the expansion of the Empire there was a growing class of people who found themselves before the bench for petty theft, hawking without a licence or prostitution. The police staff struggled to cope, and satires of the time, notably in *Punch*, revel in showing the swamping of the courts by the desperate and destitute. It is not difficult to imagine the chaos at the courts: a stream of people being brought in, and culprits in their dozens being loaded into the 'Black Marias' as they were shipped off to gaol. The missionaries squeezed in and worked when and where they could.

It was in 1876 that a printer from Hertford called Frederic Rainer, who was working as a volunteer with the Church of England Temperance Society (CETS), saw this problem at the courts and decided to act. He gave five shillings to the philanthropists who were working in a small way to help offenders. The result was a tentative placement of two missionaries in Southwark by the CETS. From there, a quiet revolution happened.

After that, two former Guardsmen, Batchelor and Nelson, became the first police court missionaries. One snippet of oral history suggests that their friendship included one episode in which Batchelor saved Nelson's life. Nelson was in the Coldstream Guards in 1861, and was discharged with good conduct in 1871. In 1877 he listed his activities, and these included visits to 438 homes, 293 attendances at police courts and 149 Temperance pledges taken. He made 117 visits to prisons and saw twenty women sent to homes.

By 1880, there were eight full-time missionaries in place and homes were opened. By 1896, there were six 'mission women' in the team, and in London these staff would interview women charged at court. Some of these were sent to an inebriates' home at Gratton Road. The service of the missionaries was best summed up by Thomas Holmes, who said, 'Sir, I cannot carry Christ in parcels and distribute him. I can only do as I think He would have done … I give them myself.'

There was someone else on the scene as well: William Wheatley. In 1887 Howard Vincent, ex-Metropolitan police officer, saw through Parliament his Probation of First Offenders Bill. This did not establish probation officers, but brought about police supervision with Home Office backing. The most significant result of this Bill was established because there was a stipulation that the offender being helped had to have a fixed 'place of abode'. In order that this could be fulfilled, Wheatley set up the St Giles Christian Mission. This was before the police court missionaries could compete with this, and Wheatley began to collect and work with young men who had committed a first offence. In 1890, a reporter from *The Daily Graphic* looked into Wheatley's work. His report included this information:

> It was not always so obvious as it is now that there are more ways of reducing crime than by merely imprisoning criminals. A great deal is left to missions such as St Giles Mission to Discharged Prisoners, with which the names of Mr George Hatton and Mr William Wheatley have been so long associated.... The headquarters of the mission are in Little Wild Street, one of those narrow and not so sweet-smelling streets leading off Drury Lane.... But Mr Wheatley is usually found elsewhere, making his round of the prisons.

The missionaries went to extremes to help the fallen, the young ones destined to be on the police Habitual Criminals Register. Thomas Holmes even offered his own house at times; he wrote that he dealt with alcoholics by giving them 'the shelter and protection' of his own home. In the context of that world of service, as Beatrice Webb talked of, the Christian wishing to take part in the active implementation of church salvation work, the precursor to a probation service was exactly what was required.

But this does not imply softness and indulgence: on the contrary, the usual statement made about the aims of probation – to 'guide, admonish and befriend' – hints at the toughness required as well as the sacrifice of time, labour and personal comfort. What was very much a help and support to the missionaries, though, was the First Offenders Act of 1886. This made it easier to give the missionaries the tasks of supervising young offenders who had been bound over; voluntary supervision was undertaken for a designated period.

All this needed cash, of course. The support was not there without finance. A typical fundraising effort was the concert given at the Bycullah Athenaeum, at Enfield, which raised a great deal of money.

The missionaries themselves were not particularly well paid – around £50 a year was average. But progress was made, and some of the main achievements of the missions are very impressive, such as the boys' shelter at Bethnal Green in 1893 in which around twenty boys would stay and be supervised for several weeks. The achievements are best appreciated with a look at some figures: in the area of what is now Greater London, missionaries visited over 5,000 homes, wrote over 3,000 letters and took more than 2,000 pledges.

The missionaries existed in the provinces as well. In Cheshire, for example, a Police Court Mission Committee was set up in 1894, created really by a clergyman, the Reverend Cogswell. Within a year, the missionaries based in Chester had been involved in 240 court cases. The first missionary employed was J.C. Porter, with a salary of £90 a year (doing much better than his London counterparts). The missions were then extended throughout the county, being established in Northwich, Altrincham and Stockport. The Chester Mission even extended its work as far as Wallasey and Broxton.

It has to be noted that not all the regions responded to opportunities to invest in this kind of probationary support: the understanding of the work done was slow to be disseminated, and of course, as it was always linked to church initiatives, there was perhaps a general feeling that things 'would just happen' left to the 'do-gooders'. In other words, there was not much in terms of organizational and corporate action to extend the work done in London in the early years. However, by 1900 there had been a definite change of gear in this respect and there were a hundred missionaries in the country by then.

In the last decades of Victorian Britain, the results of the Industrial Revolution and massive urban growth, together with huge-scale immigration into London from Eastern Europe and Russia, meant that 'everyday' minor crime spread wider and went deeper. As well as creating problems in the courts, this also added to penal issues such as the uncertainties about the prison system. In 1877, the prisons had been effectively nationalized and regimented, being run by military men. In terms of the efforts to provide help with rehabilitation, the emphasis was still on silence, reflection and hard work. Of course, until the end of the century, most local prisons had a full mix of ages, gender and category of offender nurturing what was called 'contamination' – the first-time offenders being corrupted by old lags. Until the early Edwardian years, many gaols still had women offenders inside giving birth to children.

This wider view gives us an insight into exactly how important the police court missionaries were in that social context. They reclaimed a large number of people who, without them, would have slipped into habitual crime as their only option, living in the sad and desperate underclass.

Speaking in Parliament in May 1907, Mr Herbert Samuel moved a second reading of the Probation of Offenders Bill, and he made a clear statement of its purpose:

> Its purpose was to enable Courts of Justice to appoint probation officers, and pay them salaries and fees, so that certain offenders whom the court did not think fit to imprison on account of their age, character or antecedents, might be placed on probation under the supervision of these officers.

By the time of the Act, the London Diocesan Police Court Mission had clearly shown the way in this respect. The Annual Report for 1900 reflects on the nature of their work as well as the significant achievements. It lists the work done by thirteen missionaries: they had even paid rent and lodgings for 343 people, and the total number of visits made by all the staff – to home and court – was 8,319.

There were concerns expressed about the new breed of probation officers – questions now raised that had never been raised against the 'amateurs'. Mr Stuart Worsley, Member for Sheffield Hallam, said in debate: 'What deduction was to be made from the liberty of the person who was placed under the control of a probation officer? … Would the probation officers have the right of entry into a person's house, and if not, why not? Was the officer to have the right of following a person about the country?'

One might argue that this was a very English trait: to allow the good work to go on, with magnificent achievements, but then, when it was streamlined and 'official' and within a proper system, to start asking the important questions of both a legal and a moral nature.

But the missionaries by this time were moving on. Thomas Holmes founded the Home Workers' Aid Association in 1904, and then in 1905 became a secretary with the Howard Association. Even near the end of his life he was still helping others, and with a communal aim. In 1910 he created Singholm at Walton-on-the-Naze, Essex – a holiday home in the open air for women. Holmes, Nelson, Batchelor and the others achieved amazing things in their work in the byways of London crime, and an understanding of their work gives depth and texture to any family story that involves offenders and their rehabilitation.

Thomas Holmes had special memories of some of his clients. The inebriate Jane Cakebread is one who never left his mind and imagination. He wrote of her: 'Fifty years I stood by and stood up for Jane Cakebread, and we became inseparably connected. She abused me right royally and her power of invective was superb. When she was not in prison she haunted my house and annoyed my neighbours.'

Jane told Holmes that he could be the heir to a fortune she never had, and at one time she proposed to him. She tended to recite a section from the Book of Job if a quarrel was in progress among the drunks, and Holmes noted that she patronized him 'most graciously' when he gave her a change of clothing.

This is a kind of love story, a moving account of a professional relationship that became a strange friendship. Holmes went to her funeral and never forgot her, a drunken woman of the streets. He said that 'she bestowed her affections on me'. Her death in December 1898 was reported in *The Times*: 'Jane Cakebread, who, according to official records, had been convicted 281 times for drunkenness, died on Saturday morning in Claybury Lunatic Asylum.' She had been remanded into Holloway prison 'for her state of mind to be inquired into' in January 1896.

In this short history of the missionaries, notice that mention of women is not in the mainstream narrative – but it should be. They were always there, providing the essential back-up service to the men. We have to work hard to find their presence. In an account of the missionaries' work given by Dorothy Ellison, we have this:

> missionaries are of both sexes … should always be allowed to remain. In cases of a peculiarly loathsome kind, when women are ordered out, the presence of a female missionary is valuable to give countenance to a woman, who, as prisoner or witness, would otherwise be compelled to pass through a painful ordeal in an assembly consisting solely of men.

In 1889, The Reverend Hird, working in the mission, as Martin Page recorded, wrote that 'the sole mission woman in the diocese was a mere drop in the ocean. As funds increase it is hoped that each police court missionary may have assistance of a mission woman to take up her special part in the work.' Page adds that in 1890, things were looking up in this respect: 'the CETS employed some thirty-six police court missionaries throughout the country, and Hird reported that the London Diocese now had two 'mission women'. The staff photographs in Page's history do not show any women in the lines of missionaries seated and composed, ready for their picture to be taken.

The police court missionaries were one element in a much larger picture of involvement in social welfare by the middle class, and particularly by university graduates, who saw in London poverty an opportunity to put into practice that ideal of service that Beatrice Webb had described in her autobiography (see my first chapter). Central to this initiative was Toynbee Hall, a charity that had been founded at the end of 1884 in a building of the same name at Tower Hamlets in the East End of London.

John Bew has discussed the context of this foundation: 'The social and economic status quo in Britain had begun to look unsustainable – and the political system had begun to crack.' He goes on to explain the rationale behind the Hall, and in this we see the possibility of openings for women graduates looking for work in the general ethos of the amelioration of man: 'Toynbee Hall was trying to change the debate about social welfare, and the approach to it, but it was not quite sure in which direction it should go.' But Bew adds a detail that is very relevant to the work of such people as Webb, when he provides a 'snapshot' of the Hall's activities: 'Every Tuesday evening one of the residential volunteers offered free legal advice to local people. This was particularly valuable to recent immigrants unsure of their status and rights. The assistance of Mr Western, the Poor Man's Lawyer, was widely sought.'

The element of social welfare effected by not only the Christian support workers in court, but by well-informed intellectuals with aims to develop social welfare, played a large part in providing the kind of platform needed for local probation work, as will be described later, when the work of Miss Blyth and others is discussed.

The revolution in criminal legal work brought about by the Criminal Appeal Act and the Probation of Offenders Act, both of 1907, cannot be overestimated. The intentions of the first Bill were summarized well in the list of Liberal legislation published in the Government Record (1913):

> [The Act] creates, after previous futile attempts, renewed again and again during the last sixty years, a tribunal of review in criminal cases, which places within the reach of persons convicted of crime rights of appeal similar to those enjoyed by persons who have verdicts against them in civil courts. Liberty has thus, for the first time in our law, similar safeguards to those which have long protected property.

There were to be three judges sitting on appeal, and these were High Court judges. The established concept of mercy, lodged in the Home Secretary and the Crown, still remained unchanged; it was the Secretary of State who could refer a case to appeal, as well as other channels of address through solicitors. There had been a recommendation for this as early as 1892, but the opposition was powerful and loud. Sir Henry James had tried to have such a Bill passed in 1890, and the essence of that Bill was in the text of the 1907 Act.

What this means may easily be understood today by having a cursory look at the books summarizing the appeal court records: there, cases from all over the country as well as from the Old Bailey come before the judges and arguments are heard. As we read these, every sentence takes us nearer to a statement that will either, if the case is a capital offence, end in 'sentence confirmed' or 'sentence quashed'. The reprieve of a condemned man would sometimes come after extended discussion. But, on the other hand, sometimes it took only a few minutes to confirm a sentence. Of course, many of the cases heard are not for capital offences, but it is not difficult to imagine the sense of drama and expectancy in such a court. The barrister in question, defending the plaintiff, would know that something special was needed.

The great lawyers and advocates were of course much in demand in this context. It needs to be recalled that the personality as well as the skills of the advocate were essential in the nineteenth century, when the accused could not speak. Lord Birkett wrote of one of the very best of these men, Edward Marshall Hall: 'Knowing the details of the case as I did, I listened to his every word with a fascinated wonder and amazement. When he came to his peroration and depicted the figure of justice holding the scales until the presumption of innocence was put there to turn the scale in favour of the prisoner, not only was the jury manifestly impressed, but they indeed … were under a kind of spell.'

But there was no jury in the Court of Appeal: the High Court judges were hard nuts to crack. In the early years of the court, many of the homicide cases before them were murders of wives by husbands, or lovers by the supposedly beloved. Consequently, the records of the court make compulsive reading, as every facet of human relationships is there under scrutiny.

In effect, the Act opened up many new potential aspects of a criminal career as well as to advances in the judicial system. Major villains would find themselves having more publicity, for instance. It tended to increase the public persona of the judge, and perhaps added more understanding on the part of the public about the many things a judge does in his profession. A prisoner lodging an appeal immediately becomes something other than an obscure, forgotten non-person in a cell, outside social norms; the person may have bail and be observed and reported on every time he or she walks into court. But in practical terms, it was the fear of bureaucracy and a paper mountain that deterred the legal professionals in 1907. One report said: 'There is the fact that annually some 10,000 persons are sentenced, and that theoretically each one of them may make use of the machinery of the Act.' As Shakespeare noted, the law meant 'delay', and Dickens's famous case of Jarndyce v Jarndyce in *Bleak House* reiterates that fact very strongly. It was and still is a slow process.

If we add to this the establishment of the Probation of Offenders Act of the same year, it can be seen just how much those who worked in support of the courts' processes found that a new professionalism had arrived. The possibility of appeal meant that there was much more work for those in support of the barristers in their important work of appeal – hearings that meant the difference between life and death to those who had been convicted of a capital offence. But in the Probation Act itself, there was another strand to the revolutionary year of 1907.

This Act was defined simply in the same Liberal publication: 'permits a court in suitable cases to release a child offender, or any other person, on probation, without sentencing him to fine or imprisonment; and provides for the appointment of officers to supervise and befriend such persons while on probation.'

The duties of the new staff were defined: 'to visit or receive reports from the person under supervision, to see that he observes the conditions of his recognisance, to report to the court as to his behaviour … to endeavour to find him suitable employment.'

As noted above in the discussion of the police court missionaries, there had always been women workers, in the shadowy background to the work of the Christian court workers. Now, after 1908 when the Act began to be applied, there was to be a growing number of women probation officers over the coming decades, but it took time. As Geraldine Cadbury noted in her history of juvenile offenders, 'Generally, male probation officers were in charge of men and big boys, while women, when available, were responsible for women, girls and little boys, but for years there were no women officers in many places.' They were appointed by the courts, and so there was a stress on local contacts and personalities. The training and background of recruits were not initially regulated.

It was slow and steady at first: in 1913 there was a report on the first meeting of the National Association of Probation Officers at Caxton Hall in London, which showed the public that the new profession had 'arrived'. By 1938, the Home Office had taken charge of the service, and this made the important step of making it compulsory for female probationers to be supervised by women officers. Previously, this had merely been advised.

In 1922, when probation was well established, the Home Office issued a report on the training and appointment of probation officers, and in that document there was a special mention of women: 'Women officers should be appointed as a rule to supervise women probationers, and especially qualified officers should be appointed to look after children.' One report statement stands out: 'Many persons are now employed as probation officers who are not properly qualified for the work.'

The report also focused on the educational standard of recruits and on pay. It suggested a pay scale, and of course this was unequal, biased to men. Male officers were to have not less than £200 at the age of thirty, rising to £350 when they were forty-five; women, in contrast, were to have £150 and £250 respectively. There was no statement regarding superannuation, which was considered as impracticable.

It was only a report, and therefore had to use the word *should*. This is in a very important context, as in: 'Probation is of great value as a means of reformation and is economical. Magistrates should always consider the possibility of using it.'

There is a telling insight into the attitudes to probation work and juvenile crime in the first years of the new legislation, in a letter sent to the justices' clerks at petty sessions by the Home Office. This is the most relevant passage, relating to probation: 'The Secretary of State is aware that it is difficult at the present time to find men who have time to assist as voluntary workers.... Where there are sufficient cases there should always be a paid man probation officer, with a salary sufficient to attract a fully qualified person, and a woman probation officer, to whom should be allotted all the cases of women and children.... Every effort should be made to enlist the services of ladies as volunteer workers.'

It is clear from this that there were still persisting attitudes about the ability of women to take on such demanding work, and in the area of criminal law and juveniles, although it can be seen here that the Home Secretary is trying to suggest sensitive and sensible measures, there is discrimination at work, and an obvious duality in the attitudes expressed.

Nina Blyth, who gained an OBE later, was one of the first juvenile court probation officers, appointed by the Home Office in 1915. She worked at first at the Tower Bridge Police Court, to work with a Miss Evelyn Lance. Ethel Crosland, in a memoir, wrote, 'Her office was in Old Kent Road, where she spent the whole of Saturday in order to see her working boys and girls.' Ethel Crosland began work with Nina in 1918, and Ethel refers to five other women officers at that time and just after she started work. Nina even had her own lending library for the young adults she supervised.

It appears that Evelyn Lance was the first woman officer in London, as a letter to *Probation Journal* notes. Cecil Chapman, a magistrate, wrote, 'I considered myself extremely fortunate in having for my first probation officer Evelyn Lance, who set the standard of work for a probation officer very high.' He also said of her, 'She was a natural genius in influencing children to self-mastery.'

Fortunately, thanks to scholars in the social sciences, there is some knowledge of the life and work of some of the first women probation officers. One of the most substantial archives is that of material collected by Alan Cohen, who conducted a series of interviews covering the years 1929–59. One of his interviewees, Rose Mary Braithwaite, started her career as a juvenile court probation officer in 1939, working with the London Probation Service.

Rose Mary studied at the London School of Economics and spent some time training in New York also. She later taught on a postgraduate course at Bedford College. She started her career in social work in 1939, working in a juvenile court. She explained to Alan Cohen that after 1911 Sir William Clarke Hall had worked to introduce what was then called a 'women of education' project to practise in a probationary capacity in the juvenile courts. Rose Mary explained, 'One or two [women] were appointed then and more subsequently up to '38, when the probation became a wholly public service.'

She first thought about a career in journalism, but, partly inspired by her father's work in running a club for men and boys in Limehouse, she took an increasing interest in social work. There was also a settlement near to her father's club, and so all this made her aware of extreme poverty and the need for social workers to be active in the community. She spoke about her teachers, and how they encouraged her to work at the same time as studying: 'So she sent me off to the Time and Talents Settlement in Bermondsey, where I was a disaster.'

After that, influenced by Nina Blyth, she did her first court work, and she paid tribute to Nina Blyth in the interview, saying, 'Miss Blyth gave me a tremendous lot, almost unconsciously, because she was helpful.' Then, Rose Mary's probation work began in earnest, being placed in a North London magistrates' court, and then, with a real insight into early probation work undertaken by women amongst the majority of male workers, she explained to Alan Cohen about the work with young offenders within the heart of the community: her 'office' was in a public house. She recollected, 'It was an old pub, tiny little street corner pub off East India Dock Road. Had been called The Horn of Plenty.... It was just two rooms ... like the saloon bar and the public bar.' She explained the reason for this as well: 'In those days there was this great attempt to "decriminalize" the juvenile courts. They had to meet in neutral places.'

The first real landmark since the 1922 report came in the 1938-39 reshaping of probation, following the Departmental Committee on Courts of Summary Jurisdiction in 1936. Rose Mary spoke with pride about her involvement in the burgeoning service at that time: 'You see there were only thirty-three of us in the whole of London. And I can't tell you what an elite we felt.'

In the 1950s and 1960s there were many ways in which women could be involved in social welfare, and the work of probation and of the related area of post-prison support was augmented by all kinds of social action. This was ad hoc and well-meaning, and reached into some unusual places, as is shown for instance in a move in 1962 to bring in the help of the Women's Voluntary Service in relation to borstal. A newsletter from the WVS in September of that year explains the thinking:

> One of the biggest problems in the aftercare of borstal boys is that of finding suitable accommodation for those who cannot live at home. Well-run hostels are in short supply and satisfactory lodgings are hard to find in the big cities, even for people with good recommendations. In any case, these boys who have been away from normal society for so long really need something more than an impersonal landlady who is only too glad that they should be out of the house during their leisure hours.

The newsletter appeals to women to be involved and adds, 'We feel that we need the help of some of our very experienced ex-overseas members in this scheme, because we know that they are used to being "mum" and to listening wisely to problems covering all aspects of life.'

There is a wonderful irony in this, if it is recalled that almost a century before, a similar crusade into social welfare had been undertaken with the element of ingrained amateurism of the English way of doing things. That spirit of finding solutions outside the system was alive and well at the same time that probation itself was in flux, and slowly becoming more accepted as an important profession.

After the war, women probation officers settled into the new shaping of the service, and as time went on, issues relating to the profession became more general rather than specifically related to that work. In 1989, Michelle Hayes wrote a feature on what was a hot topic everywhere really, where women stood alongside men: the notion of women's under-representation in management. Hayes argued that in the probation service, there was reluctance on the part of women to apply for promotion. She wrote, 'We know that whilst women and men are represented in more or less equal numbers at main grade level, their numbers decline rapidly at SPO [senor probation officer] level.... The same pattern arises in Social Services departments.'

Hayes suggests that there was a perception of 'direct discrimination' and that the strain of having multiple roles in society needed to be alleviated. She suggested the heart of the problem: 'Facilities for maternity leave, job-sharing and part-time work, for example, offer some help to women.'

Another important aspect of the work of women officers is the need they have, according to Hayes, to 'operate in accordance with their own system of values' – meaning that they need relational activities with clients, rather than a deep involvement with mechanistic tasks. Hayes adds, 'This is evidenced by women's comments about their dislike of administration and paperwork and their major concern about losing contact with clients.'

Michele Hayes's article typifies the debate on problems relating to women working in the criminal justice system in the decades after the war. Whereas in the early years of the probation service, women had mainly chosen to devote themselves to the 'idea of service', as expressed by Beatrice Webb, as time went on, the debate that is now familiar in all areas of work – 'having it all' in terms of home, family and career – began to intensify.

Probation work, linked to the operation of the juvenile courts, was very prominent in the media and in all locations where debate took place, right through the twentieth-century, but before the Second World War, the juvenile court took centre stage in this respect, as there was extensive interest in publications and in legislation on the subject. Geraldine Cadbury, for instance, a writer who was also a JP, wrote a plea for the special considerations needed in dealing with youngsters facing the court: 'Both probation officers and representatives of the Education Committee want seats, as do witnesses, but the fewer persons present, the better.' She placed probation firmly in the centre of interest: 'Probation is the sheet anchor of the modern juvenile court and should be used in all suitable cases if the home is a possible one.'

In addition to the probation workers, there is an array of other legal occupations, and naturally, their titles and job descriptions change over time. In the 1960s, for instance, across the range of criminal courts, from the House of Lords to a magistrates' court, the officials were: justices' clerk, clerk of the peace, associate of the High Court, clerk of assize, registrar of Court of Appeal and registrar of the Clerk of the Parliaments.

One white-collar occupation of special interest here is that of justices' clerk. The origin of the office is in the personal assistants used by county magistrates, centuries past, and such a person needed a good knowledge of the law. After 1847, when the massive increase in cases handled at petty sessions meant that justices needed more reliable advice, the position of petty sessional clerk was established. A century later, according to Sir Thomas Skyrme, 'The position of clerk [was] one of dignity and the holding of that position may itself be regarded as part of the reward.' The Justices' Clerks Society, formed in 1903, worked for regulation and professional standards, and gradually, as Skyrme explains, there was a considerable advance in their status and ambitions: 'The clerks' most interesting achievement was their invasion of the Stipendiary Magistracy.' This is because an Act of 1949 opened up the possibility that justices' clerks could become stipendiaries. The latter were barristers, paid for the work, as opposed to the lay magistrates on the bench. A notable stepping stone in this respect is the appointment of L.M. Pugh as stipendiary for Huddersfield; he had been clerk to the Sheffield justices.

For a long time before 1949, though, there had been heated discussion on the matter of appointment. In the Justices' Clerk Act of 1877, the stipulations for appointment were that the applicant had to be a barrister, a solicitor or a clerk who had served seven years at a petty sessional court. By the turn of the century, after the formation of the Clerk's Society in 1903, it was clear that there was a more flexible attitude in some areas. A report from the Law Society noted in 1915: 'Several provincial law societies are now deprecating the growing practice of appointed laymen to the post of justices' clerk. The Council of the Law Society ruled that the 1877 Act should be followed according to the letter.'

These clerkships had been a male preserve from the beginning. Women entered the profession in the 1940s, and that fact alone immediately shows how far the white-collar supporting roles in law were behind the Bar itself in the admittance of women. First, Miss L.M. Holland was appointed at Stowmarket in 1944, and then in 1947, Miss Joan Adair started work at Kingston-upon-Thames as the first full-time clerk.

There are also the solicitors' clerks – an occupation Charles Dickens once had; they were the office workers behind solicitors, and they had to have some knowledge of the law, of course. As time went on, their roles became more and more demanding, and today they are within the membership of the Chartered Institute of Legal Executives. This professional organization began in 1963, sanctioned by the Law Society, in order to provide professional training for solicitors' clerks. On their database today, the listings show that members are predominantly women.

Chapter 8

The 'Lady Detectives'

In one or two cases we have been informed that women have been instrumental in securing evidence in cases of serious crime.

Home Office, Report on Detective Work, 1938

Before focusing on the women detectives in the last seventy years, an outline of the development of the detective work and training in Britain since c1930 is needed. The modern story begins with a man called Trenchard.

Air Marshal Hugh Trenchard was Commissioner of the Metropolitan Police for just five years, from 1931-35. He had served in the Boer War and in Ireland. He had been Commander of the Royal Flying Corps in the Great War and then played a major role in the creation of the RAF. His regime in the police brought about many radical changes, including bringing in a statistical department and a Daily Crime Telegram; he created a Detective Training School and a Police Scientific Laboratory. These were both adjuncts of the Hendon College. The Training School at Hendon was his work too. He was confident that his reforms were beneficial and looked at the areas of police work that were arguably most in need of radical changes. He also challenged the policy, going back to the beginnings with Peel, of promoting from within. Trenchard saw the virtues of a short-service scheme.

What Trenchard did was make the Police College the place where the real 'career men' would be trained and encouraged to use their talents, and to offer finite career periods to others. A short-term contract would allow a recruit to sign on for just ten years before retiring with a gratuity payment. His short-lived regime was assured some kind of continuance, however, as he appointed Sir Philip Game to succeed him – a man who could be relied on to act as if he were still an aide-de-camp.

What happened in terms of detective work was that the world's first training programme was begun in 1936 on the Hendon Police College Estate. By the Metropolitan Police Act of 1933, Hendon was established as the centre for police training. It was opened in 1934 and it was clearly an institution that became indispensable, and after being closed for the duration of the war, its work was resumed but with a different name: The Metropolitan Police Training School.

We have memoirs about how men became detectives and these explanations help us to understand what the motivations were. The middle line in this was discontentment with the beat work of the 'ordinary copper'. Leonard Nipper Read, for instance, 'the man who caught the Krays', explains it in that way, and explains that the course at Hendon Police College, which he attended in 1947, was 'drilling and lectures on public order, diseases of animals, child neglect, company fraud, incest, rape, bigamy, sodomy, helping children at school crossings, suicide, infanticide, drunks, ponces and traffic control'. Read started as a detective when a senior officer said he had a job for him and that he would be working in plain clothes.

Before the new training, though, a bright policeman – or a restless one – followed a set procedure of application to become a detective. This is explained in a biography of Nixon, later Detective Inspector, and the method was outlined by a senior officer:

> He outlined the routine. An applicant wrote his name in the book provided for the purpose in the station. In due course, as vacancies occurred, if he were considered by the station detective sergeant as a possibility his name was forwarded through the usual channels and he was interviewed by the divisional detective inspector. If the interview was satisfactory the applicant was posted for CID duties as an 'aide' when he was tried out on his own.

Read was a man who went through that process twenty years later, and he explains that as an aide the idea is that you have a mentor. He began at St John's Wood and there his mentor was Martin Walsh, of whom Read wrote: 'I was put under the wing of one of the best detectives I have ever met.… He was an older man, in his forties, who was used as a 'tutor' aide. He taught me what investigating was all about.' In that way, Nixon and Read learned to be detectives by working on the streets with experienced men. But what about the new men going to the college?

A great deal can be learned about that curriculum from the 1938 Report of the Departmental Committee on Detective Work and Procedure. That report outlines the whole course of training, from a review of general detective work, through to specific skills such as crime record keeping and photography. The document was produced by a team led by Sir Samuel Hoare, Secretary of State for the Home Office. In terms of commentary on existing detective work, the report puts considerable emphasis on communication between individual officers and indeed at the group operational level, as in comments about detectives from different forces gathering to exchange information at race meetings. Men asked in the course of the enquiry had repeatedly suggested that detective work would be notably improved if a 'spirit of co-operation was fostered'.

The 1930s was the time at which it was properly registered that liaison across the country was becoming crucially important in police work. The report recommends bringing senior officers from different forces together so that they can work together at the earliest opportunity in the process of investigating a specific crime. The normal practice at the time, if a man had to go to work in another area, was for the officer to notify the CID concerned but the report's authors noted a very uneven application of this principle. They advised individual procedures, but stressed that an effective system of intelligence about criminals was at the top of the list of requirements. In the years immediately before the 1938 report, 'lending' of officers had been very small scale, and it is clear that these instances were for particular expertise; just twenty lendings took place in the years from 1931 to 1936. Naturally, in murder cases, this kind of lending activity is more important, and the authors report that the recent results were encouraging:

> In the five years 1931-35 there were known to the police 460 cases of murder or suspected murder of persons aged one year or over [others were infanticide since 1922]. In 181 of these cases the murderer ... committed suicide, leaving 279 cases to be detected.... Arrests were made in 254 cases.

Training of officers received close attention. After all, numbers of officers were accelerating quickly and the force was huge compared to the men at work in the Ripper years five decades before this. In 1938 there were 1,198 CID personnel; Liverpool and Birmingham had equivalent forces of over a hundred men. As recruitment was clearly increasing, it was a good time to take stock of needs and of methods. All the obvious issues were discussed in the course of exploring the nature of the detective needed in that time of inter-war expansion of organized crime, rackets and robberies. One of the central points considered was the idea of a probationary period, the line of thought parallel to the 'aide' system. The panel concluded that no probation was needed but conceded that a detective is 'always on probation' in that he or she must always be 'subject to continuing to discharge duties successfully'.

The syllabus for training recommended in the report was based on the question of integration or separation from the normal police training syllabus. The decision was that a thirteen-week course was necessary for detective recruits. In addition, the decision was for recruits to spend six weeks attached to a CID as in the aide system. In terms of the content of the syllabus, this is, in summary form, the course decided on:

Week 1 Conduct and professionalism; dealing with the press; prevention of crime; co-operative detective work; use of scientific aids; intelligence reports; local knowledge; observation and special contexts for work.

Week 2 Fingerprints; judges' rules; telephone and wireless; use of cars; photography; searching scene of crime.
Week 3 Legal knowledge – summonses; warrants; powers of arrest; identification parades; prisoners' rights; larceny; receivers; housebreaking notation and study of scene; robbery.
Week 4 Sexual offences; knowledge of obscene publications; infanticide.
Week 5 Homicide law; scene of crime photography; coroners and inquests; wounds; blood groups; poisoning; explosives offences; arson; financial fraud and fraud in use of materials.
Week 6 Bribery and corruption; blackmail; Official Secrets Acts; procedure in courts; reports to other forces.
Week 7 Dangerous drugs; courts; extradition.
Week 8 Depositions; dying declarations; testimony of the sick.

This is, as would be expected, very thorough and wide ranging. Police work expands and becomes more complex as population increases and the knock-on effects of industrial and urban growth continue. At the time of that report, all manner of recent developments were absorbed into the thinking behind the syllabus. To take one example: the first Official Secrets Act was passed in 1911 but there had been a second one in 1920 and a third was in preparation as this report was written, to become statute law the next year, 1939. A detective would have to become acquainted with such topics as knowing which places were prohibited and why, and to whom; how communication of classified information could or would be passed; and how to access accommodation addresses of suspects. Another example of the complexity and also the delicacy of the knowledge absorbed is the awareness of the 'dying declaration'. It was not uncommon, in the age well before motorways, for a police officer to find him or herself in an ambulance on the way to hospital with a dying victim of a murderous attack. The dying declaration would be crucially important and would need to be written carefully verbatim. In one case, an old man had been beaten almost to death by two assailants in a lonely farmhouse; he talked in the ambulance to the police officer about the attackers' accents, saying they sounded Chinese. That detail led to a string of events in the ensuing investigation.

One very important topic approached by the report was the ongoing issue of records. There were, of course, ever-growing records in all counties and areas and the authors of the report saw the central importance of this being rationalized and also unified in terms of method and control. It might have been stating the obvious, but the point was made that 'It is important that the functions of the Criminal Record Office should not be assumed by any regional record centre' and that a Main Fingerprint Index should be maintained. The Clearing House system would be maintained and reviewed, in order to make sure that the right information was directed to the right place.

What about the more people-centred aspects of the new detective work? One of the most enlightening examples of this is in the details about photography in the report. An appendix goes into specific detail about what procedure and knowledge the detective using photography for records must have. There are technical drawings of all equipment and very particular images of the chair on its turntable. The basis of this work is the maintenance of the card index record. This had ten sections of information to be listed in the right places. After that, there are seven categories of index described. If we add to this the expected knowledge of publications and the updating of basic criminological knowledge, then the work of the detective could easily become 'paperwork', so we have to ask about the supposed excitement and appeal of the profession at that time. The answers are in a study by Percy Hoskins, referred to previously. In his richly illustrated guide to detective training as it was around 1955, Hoskins gives a clear idea of how that conception in the report of twenty years earlier had become a workable system. His book, *No Hiding Place*, is a feel-good advert for Scotland Yard but it explains all the intricacies of the work for the layperson.

Hoskins's hypothetical detective recruit begins with his thirteen weeks at Peel House, the new training venue after the Second World War. He then becomes a detective recruit for a year, and then to Hendon. The basis is practical all the way: 'The paramount need for keen observation is again drilled into the men's heads. The theory of the Yard is that a good description is better than any picture and its detectives are taught to cultivate retentive memories as a matter of routine.' Then the recruit is faced with the more academic side of work – criminal law, for instance. The practice then was for both senior detectives and lawyers working in prosecution.

Hoskins interviewed Commander Rawlings, Deputy of the CID about detective work and the reply was, 'It is 95 per cent perspiration, 3 per cent inspiration and 2 per cent luck!' On top of all the good advice and legal material, the college was equipped with every kind of device for simulation of events as possible, and every aid for information processing. These were such items as subject maps, study of facial characteristics, observation tests, use of scale models, anatomy, basic ballistics and forgery methods.

As for the more modern concepts and elements of detective work, some of the principal ones were around in the 1950s but not in operation or even generally accepted. For instance, offender profiling was conceived by Dr James Brussel in 1956 after a bomb explosion in a cinema in Brooklyn. It was the work of a criminal dubbed 'The Mad Bomber'. During the war, Brussel had worked with the CIA and the FBI on profiling. He then studied case notes and went to work on the profile. The doctor listed ten important features of the criminal, including the note that the man had 'an Oedipus complex'. Sure enough, a man was tracked down after a phone call.

But for more practical, people-centred detective skills, one of the most criticized elements of training has been interviewing technique. This situation has been exacerbated by prominent murder cases in which suspects who have emerged as mentally ill or with learning deficiencies have produced 'confessions' after interviewing. One remarkable case was in 1946, when two Scotland Yard detectives came north to the Lincolnshire area and interviewed a man who was a murder suspect. His housekeeper had been battered to death and investigation had opened up no other potential suspects. He was mentally at the age of fifteen, yet a quite sophisticated confession (in linguistic terms) was produced. But for a talented and strong-willed barrister, the man would quite probably have been hanged.

It is obvious to anyone studying detective procedure in recent years – even simply watching police interviews on television – that women detectives have a special ability and usefulness in the interview room during an investigation.

Training began in some old huts in Hendon. By 1973, Hendon was used again after a spell at Peel House in Knightsbridge. Obviously, training today has a high level of technology involved, but a report published in *Police Review* in June 2006 indicates that the CID is no longer seen as a glamorous job and new strategies are being used to attract recruits. Certainly, back in 1936 there was an appeal of glamour, but Hoskins's work relies heavily on the appeal of some of the features that had made life in the services appealing to many in the war: such things as advanced communications, fast cars, efficient fire power, physical confrontation and, of course, a sense of a moral crusade against the 'forces of evil and anarchy' as textualized in magazines and comics.

Making the detectives in the years c1930 to 1960 meant a constant series of revisions of method, habits, ways of working and, most of all, in the personnel – the types of men who came along at the right time to use their talents well. The next step was logically to take the CID more efficiently out of 'the Smoke' and into the regions, and that is where we will meet Leonard Nipper Read again. The strictures in the 1930s about more efficient communication with the regional forces gradually attained more importance. The old cry of 'Send for Scotland Yard' became more and more common as crime turned more violent and ruthless in the burgeoning new towns and the troubled Victorian ones. That call had been going on in a sense even before there was a Scotland Yard – since 1834, when people from a village in Wiltshire asked for help from 'Bow Street'. A pattern was established, and it is almost mythic. First there is a murder or a high-level robbery; then the local police do all the traditional things but are baffled. Clearly, the more sophisticated officers in London will help, so call them in. Even the amateurs in fiction were called out for local horrors, the pattern being, arguably, Sherlock Holmes going out to Dartmoor to sort out the ravages caused by the Hound of the Baskervilles.

So, what part were women to play in all this?

Long before there were real female detectives, there were fictional ones, and we have to ask why such figures captured – and still capture – the popular imagination, and attract writers of crime fiction or television crime drama. In 1864, a novel called *The Female Detective*, by Andrew Forrester, was published. The sleuth in question, Miss Gladden, tells the reader at one point: 'Without going into particulars, the reader will comprehend that the woman detective has far greater opportunity than a man of intimate watching and keeping her eyes upon matters near which a man could not conveniently play the eavesdropper.' That is a valid point, but it was to take another century before the real woman detective was to be as prominent and active as Miss Gladden.

Long before they actually existed, the female sleuths had a special kind of attraction to storytellers in popular culture, and the reasons for this are diverse and complex. Perhaps the main source of interest comes from the fact that, in the Victorian period, such a role was utterly out of all comprehension when the dominant ideology placed woman firmly in the home, as mother and wife. For a woman to move into the realm of what we now call 'male adventure' in fiction was a stunning, unsettling and, of course, quite intriguing thought.

Just before Forrester's book, in 1861, there was *Experiences of a Lady Detective* featuring Mary Paschal, a novel in the so-called 'yellow back' series of popular crime fiction. Peter Haining, in his history of the genre, notes, writing about the publishers, George Vickers, that their concept was immensely successful and explains why: 'The idea that the texts were written by real detectives was used to enhance their appeal. Whether Mary Paschal had any basis in fact or not, she is undoubtedly a worthy pioneer of crime fiction. Aged about forty, she is described as having taken up her occupation as a result of her husband's sudden death, which left her penniless.'

The irony of that concept would not have been lost on the Victorian readers, as so many independent women had to invent reasons for their enterprise as single individuals, outside a family ethos: even Elizabeth Gaskell's 'undone' heroine in her novel *Ruth* (1853), though merely a seamstress, has to invent a dead husband to keep herself morally sound.

This early status of the woman detective is important in any history of the profession. From the first, the woman detective has been a singular role model for women aspiring to be equal to men in the ideology of tough police work – the hard, uncompromising sleuth, like Philip Marlowe, dealing with the 'mean streets' and coping with all shades of immorality, was essentially male. Then the women police arrived, and they were seen as astoundingly bold, daring and 'modern'. This image is still there in contemporary police dramas and films.

Women detectives, in the professional sense, began in the staff of the famous Pinkerton Detective Agency in the US in the nineteenth century. The agency employed several women, and the first was Kate Warne. She was a widow, who was recruited in 1856, and in the plot against Lincoln's life that was hatched in 1861, before the successful assassination in Washington, Kate Warne played a major role. The Pinkertons infiltrated an anti-Union cell in Baltimore, and when Lincoln went through the city, Pinkerton himself, and Warne, accompanied him in the 'parlour car' and all was well.

When Kate was asked why she would be a successful detective, she gave the answer that dominated thinking about women detectives much later, in Scotland Yard. She said, as Graham Nown explained, 'that she could worm out secrets in many places to which it was impossible for male detectives to gain access.'

Kate Warne, and other women later employed by Pinkerton, had shown the world that women could have particular uses in detective work, but it was to be a very long time after the 1860s before Britain acknowledged that fact.

One particular aspect of crime always invited the participation of women in detective work: prostitution. In this context, they were always required as ancillary workers, and as the feminine element in such activities as dealing with suicides along the Thames, or working with lost children and strays. Then, when the notion of 'white slavery' became a hot topic for the media, notably in the first three decades of the twentieth-century, these women in the constabulary had a role.

In 1885, W.T. Stead, the writer and journalist, bought a young girl for £5 in order to show how easy it would be for a man to sexually exploit and abuse a female child. He went to prison for this, but the topic of child prostitution was the subject of a campaign at the time by the *Pall Mall Gazette*, on the theme of 'The Maiden Tribute of Modern Babylon' – using the image of the old myth of the minotaur, who grabbed and ate maidens who were sacrificed to him. As Christopher Howse wrote, 'White slavery was the banner for 1885 – more particularly underage prostitution. It was something Parliament had been half-heartedly addressing since 1881.'

This led to the Criminal Law Amendment Act of 1885, which led to a result summarized neatly by H.G. Cocks in his history of the personal column: 'In other words, "good girls" were protected by law, but "bad girls" had to look after themselves.'

By the 1920s, there were prominent cases that highlighted the exploitation of young women, as in the Morriss Case of 1925, which sprang from an advert in *The Times* that read: 'Young girl of gentle birth required to look after large dogs in the country. Live in. Experience unnecessary. Common sense essential.' This case provides a template for the process involved: the wealthy man would use a female friend or relative to meet the young girls who applied, and then, after a seemingly innocent and normal introduction to the employment advertised, the man would make sexual advances to the young applicants. In other words, it was procurement, deception and often sexual attack or rape. Morriss was given a longish prison sentence. As this kind of crime was easily effected, it involved police work increasingly, and women police officers were needed. It involved undercover work and also a high level of sensitivity and tact, of course.

But as in the case of Lilian Wyles at the CID, explained in Chapter 3, most work was, in normal circumstances, confined to working with women and children, and statement taking. However, war was not part of normal circumstances.

There were several important advances in detective work during and soon after the Second World War. In 1940, identikit was in its early phase of development, initiated by Hugh MacDonald. In 1941, the murder case of Rachel Dobkins was solved after work done on dental identification, and in 1953, television viewers saw the image of the first crime suspect on their screens. In the same year, the celebrated discovery of DNA by Crick and Watson provided the first step towards its application in forensics, although it was another forty years before it brought about a conviction. This was an exciting time to be a detective, so were women playing a part in the work at that time? The answer is, only to a very limited extent.

In 1938, the report quoted in the epigraph to this chapter, in the course of 500 pages devoted to detective recruitment, practice and training, devoted just over half a page to the topic of women detectives. There is a slight tone of paternalistic resentment in the wording:

> In one or two cases we have been informed that women have been instrumental in securing evidence in cases of serious crime.... We recognize that women can be, and in some forces are, employed with advantage in some varieties of detective inquiries, as apart from observation work in plain clothes, and in various branches of clerical work in CID headquarters offices.

The Victorian notion of 'separate spheres' was alive and well in the nation's police force. There was not even the faintest whiff of women doing any of the more dramatic, physical side of the work, let alone the intellectual element. In fact, the conclusion reached by the authors of the report was, 'We have not found sufficient evidence of any special need for the employment of policewomen as detective officers, or of their special aptitude for this work.' They did not recommend any departure from the present attitude, which was to grudgingly accept that women in CID should stay in secondary, supportive roles.

By 1940, the recommendations of the 1938 report appear to have been ignored, because *The Times* announced that 'In consequence of the successful use of women police officers of the Metropolitan Force in detective work, the Home Office has authorized an increase in the branch from 140 to 150.' Women really came into their own as detectives in wartime. A press report on the new recruits explains: 'The cunning which characterized the campaign of violence of members of the illegal IRA led authorities to employ women police officers, many of whom were able to shadow Irish suspects without themselves being noticed. When they gave evidence in courts their names were carefully suppressed.'

Women detectives had also been used in tracing aliens. The new women officers were to be 'utilized in all types of criminal investigation' and, astoundingly, they were to have equal pay and allowances to that of men.

In fact, this situation was very similar to the espionage undertaken by women in the Great War. These women worked in the spy-catching section of the War Office, and Tammy Proctor explains their work:

> These women (and teenage girls) worked alongside male civil servants, military personnel and special secret service officers at the London MI5 HQ.... As clerks, supervisors, report writers, translators, printers, searchers, messengers, and historians, women made it possible for a tiny spy-tracking office ... to become a massive information clearing house.

The police situation in 1940 could be described as parallel to that, with women working as detectives, their skills and nature applied where there was most obvious use and benefit.

However, as detectives they were also useful in more everyday wartime situations, such as working against pickpockets and bag snatchers and other common crime. As one report describes, there was some front-line detective work:

> One of them [women detectives] was recently called upon to carry out duties of a dangerous kind in an effort to track down motor bandits. Acting on instructions, she stood alone on the pavement in the blackout waiting for thieves using a motor car to snatch her handbag, while her male colleagues remained hidden. The ruse failed through the carelessness of a member of the public, but the woman officer demonstrated her capacity for detective work, and has since been employed on many inquiries requiring tact, resource and ability.

At the same time that Scotland Yard was employing women detectives slightly more widely, women 'private eyes' were there – although thin on the ground. During the Second World War, the magazine *Tit-Bits* had a feature on a Mrs May Greenhalgh and, as Graham Nown wrote in his history of detectives, 'Mrs Greenhalgh, a middle-aged mother of six, had been sleuthing for twenty years by the time *Tit-Bits* discovered her…. Her bread and butter work was gleaning evidence for divorce, with a few commercial clients on the side.'

There was more than simply watching adulterous people in action; she had a penchant for disguise. As Graham Nown adds, she 'had a disguise wardrobe which would have done justice to a music-hall entertainer.' (See plate 22)

Throughout the last half century there have been radical changes in outlook, police practice and in the nature of crimes, of course. Basically, the sheer numbers of new crimes now on the statute book have meant that women detectives have been involved in a more diverse range of crimes. But it has been slow in coming. In 1962, for instance, Scotland Yard announced that some women constables would be selected for detective training, and would be offered a ten-week training course. They were to be appointed as aides and would have to serve a year in plain clothes as well as the official training. But only five years later, the reading public, in a survey of crime fiction, were amazed to learn that no women ever headed murder investigations, as there were none of a sufficiently high rank.

In the 1970s little changed for women detectives in terms of their main duties, as the case of a male stripper and club owners arrested in

1976 shows. Two women detectives had watched the performance, in plain clothes, and then made the arrests. This perhaps signalled a new toughness, and a step nearer to their being equally at home in male as well as in female contexts in police work. In fact, by 1983, the television series featuring two American women detectives, *Cagney and Lacey*, was considered by American audiences to show women being 'too butch' whereas it appears that British viewers had no such criticisms.

In 1986, Norman Lucas published the first book to provide a wide survey of the spectrum of work undertaken by women detectives in Britain: *WPC 'Courage'*. Here, he provides case studies of women working undercover on sex and drugs cases and gives vivid accounts of police operations in which the women officers were engaged on perilous work. The stories sometimes read with the same level of drama and excitement as a Hollywood movie, as when DCI Carole Scard went undercover to gather information about a drugs dealer. She arrived at his flat, under the guise of being a potential purchaser of the flat, and while there, a villain who knew Scard turned up at the door to pay a social call. She recalled the contact made by the man the next day: 'The following morning proved me right. He telephoned me. In our business, there has to be a certain amount of give and take with criminals. There was just no way that I would have been alive and at my desk that morning, had he not kept his mouth shut.'

Carole Scard was also involved in Operation Cyril, which was a plan to thwart a smuggling gang on the Cornish coast in 1979. A large team of officers was at work on this case, which stretched back a long time previously, when it had been noted that runs were being made by a trawler to destinations that had nothing to do with fishing. The result was that Carole was posted at the 'front line', as it were, sleeping overnight in a car on the beach, after chatting up the locals, spinning them a story about her assumed identity, and her reason for being there.

She told Lucas about the moment of real danger, and Lucas wrote, 'On the third night of her stay, a group of men became curious. When darkness replaced the sunlight of the warm September days in 1979 they waited until after midnight and then shone their torches through the car windows, to confirm that the fascinating female … really was so hard up that the vehicle really was her bedroom.' Carole Scard told Lucas 'how her heart thumped when the beams from the torches illuminated the inside of her car.'

Some of the women detectives of those years really did lead lives as dangerous and risky as those depicted in the television dramas. Take Inspector Susan Chapman, for instance, who was working in Boston, in plain clothes, after a drug dealer. The night led to a violent punch-up: 'Tablets were thrown across the hall and we ended up fighting. My boyfriend was hit over the head with a bottle and there was blood everywhere. The youth I held bit and punched me and in the struggle, we fell through a door into the kitchen. As we fought, pots and pans were everywhere.'

There is no doubt that in the last few decades, women detectives have worked in particular roles that compare very much with those of their male counterparts. Equal status and equal career opportunities bring with them equal danger and very high demands on personal strength, energy and determination in the very difficult work our police personnel do every day.

Chapter 9

Sheriffs, Lord Lieutenants and Coroners

Their law is the true embodiment
Of everything that is excellent
It has no kind of fault or flaw
And I, my Lords, embody the law …

W.S. Gilbert, *Iolanthe*

The structure of the British legal system has so many offices, with professional mixed with amateur, and with archaic terminology still surviving, that the layperson could be forgiven for being confused by the proliferation of job descriptions in the law, from local up to the very top of its administration. To many, it might seem that the law is more concerned with dressing and looking powerful than it is with the everyday concerns of the individual trying to understand the complexities of the legal framework. But of course, the concept of law has to have a material presence, showing in no uncertain terms that it is mighty and that it is something that regulates the notion of transgression.

Nowhere is this ceremony and show of power more evident than in the ancient offices of High Sheriff and Lord Lieutenant.

In the television drama *Downton Abbey*, the lord of the manor hated to be left out of the military activity and the rush to find a uniform that were instigated by the arrival of the Great War. In no time at all he was in a very dignified outfit – as Lord Lieutenant of the county. This has been an important honorary office for a very long time, defined by the law dictionaries as a principal legal officer for a county 'appointed for the purpose of mustering the inhabitants for the defence of the country. The Lord Lieutenant of a county was in general to be appointed president of the County Territorial Association.' This was a significant role in times of any threat of invasion, of course, but what about more general legal applications? There was one important role indeed: he or she made recommendations for the appointment of magistrates.

Today there are thirty-four women Lord Lieutenants in England, and if the question is asked as to how a person becomes such a dignified and important figure, then a look at two women Lieutenants and their work is helpful.

Jennifer, Baroness Gretton's life will answer the question. She was born in 1943, in Cornwall. In the family estate in Leicestershire, she has been prominent in charity and community work for some time. In addition, she served as a Justice of the Peace, and then was given an honorary Doctor of Laws degree. It seems a natural progression from that status to the Lord Lieutenant position in Leicestershire, which she took in 2003, after two years of being the Deputy Lieutenant.

Similarly, Dame Janet Trotter was also born in 1943 and was an academic in her main career, being a lecturer at Winchester, followed by Vice Principal of Lancaster and then Principal of St Paul and St Mary's College, Cheltenham. She has also had national positions: chair of the Council of Church Colleges and Universities, and has worked in the higher administration of the NHS in Gloucestershire.

She was appointed Lord Lieutenant of Gloucestershire in 2010.

In 1883 there was an execution in Lincoln Prison. James Anderson, of Owston Ferry in Lincolnshire, had murdered his wife, Mary. As with all hangings, there had to be an official record, and that included those present on that fateful day. The document records warders, medical officer, local reporters, and two other persons, described as 'Under Sheriff' and 'Sheriff's Officer'. Clearly, this was an event with a high level of ritual, and it would seem to anyone reading this, that the sheriff simply officiates at such functions. But there is more to it than that.

Today, there are still high sheriffs, as they are properly known, and they have their officers. In 2015 there were fourteen women sheriffs in England and Wales, from a total of fifty-five. The principal duties of the office today are to 'lend support to the principal organs of the constitution within their county – the Royal Family, the judiciary, the police and other law enforcement agencies', as the literature of the High Sheriffs' Association states. Add to this the attendance on judges of the crown courts, help where required in the voluntary sector and support the Lord Lieutenant, and it can be seen that there is more to the post than ceremony.

The term derives from the term 'shire reeve' in the medieval period, and goes back to pre-Norman times. In the earlier centuries, it was a position entailing considerable everyday powers and responsibilities, but in 1887, The Sheriffs' Act, which is still in force, established that the position lasted for one year, and was in the hands of the monarch. The most expressive signification of the office today is surely the remarkable dress. This includes a white and yellow 18-carat gold chain, a black velvet coat, sword and cocked hat. The most striking, and very dashing feature is the lace jabot worn around the neck.

In early times, the sheriff was appointed by the sovereign, but with advice from a permanent council. But there was more to it, as one writer on county sheriffs explains: 'The sheriffdom might be the inheritance of a private family. Normally, the sheriff received a commission from the crown, the king's choice being guided by the advice of one or more of his great officers.' There is a very long list of sheriffs, of course, and this has always been kept and updated by the Controller of Her Majesty's Stationery Office.

Before the nineteenth century, there had been a steady reduction in their powers; they had some powers taken away, such as the function of tax collection, but naturally they were always in demand as a symbolic figurehead to the law in the shires.

Throughout the years in which the assize court circuits were in operation, the sheriff was responsible for the hospitality and accommodation given to the judges on circuit. This meant that a measure of ceremony, style and panache went with the work. In Lincoln, for instance, outside the castle (where the assize court was situated within the grounds) there is a beautiful building that was the special living accommodation for the judges. In the workings of the assize system, they were important. As the description of their work as stated by the High Sheriffs' Association, this was that, 'The sheriff remained responsible for issuing writs, having ready the court, prisoners and juries, and then executing the sentences once they were pronounced.'

In the 1920s, there was a certain noticeable level of discussion on the office. A feature in *The Times* summarized the current situation: 'The office of high sheriff is now unpaid, and may indeed involve the holder in considerable expenditure, although certain expenses are met by the Treasury.' He adds that in the late Middle Ages, 'contributions towards the expenses of the High Sheriff were made by the magistrates and leading men of the county, and down to the nineteenth century one of the incidents of the assizes was "riding with the Sheriff", in which the local dignitaries brought wine and food.' In 1922, when that was written, the sheriff's duties were still regulated by laws dating back to 1328, consolidated under the Sheriff's Act of 1887.

There was a certain level of negative discussion on the office of sheriff in the years after the Second World War, and in 1971, as Basil Nield recalls, there was a meeting called by Captain Jeremy Elwes, High Sheriff of Lincolnshire at the time, 'to launch what *The Times* called "a campaign to preserve the oldest office of the English crown".' Nield goes on to explain what developed:

> At this conference in London the High Shrievalty Association was formed to save the office of High Sheriff from disappearing when the Crown Court should replace the old assize and quarter sessions courts. A leading article in *The Times* was headed, 'What will High Sheriffs do then?'

The oldest secular dignity under the crown survived.

Perhaps because of Robin Hood, the best known sheriff is that of Nottingham, and indeed that city had its female sheriff in 2012, in the person of Joan Casson. She was interviewed by Allen Wright, and her biography helps the layperson to understand how a particular individual becomes High Sheriff. She explains, 'I was elected to the Nottingham City Council in 1995 and have been Vice Chair of the Environment Committee and Chair of Licensing Committee.' Her account of her work expands the usual profile: she explained that she had a role in developing citizenship and enhancing pride in the local community. She added, 'I also feel proud as a woman to hold this role, a role that many people stereotypically view as a preserve of a white male!'

In the three months that Joan was in office at the time of the interview, she had acted as a cultural ambassador, visiting the city's twin at Karlsruhe in Germany and meeting some children from Belarus. Obviously, the office is expanding its scope. When asked about her infamous predecessor, she replied, 'Today's sheriff is basically a good character who is trying to redress the balance!'

The first woman sheriff was Mrs Foster Welch, who took the post in Southampton in 1926. She was a member of the British Fascist Party and was a candidate for them in that city in 1927, at a time when there were 100,000 members of the Fascist Party in Britain. She was a remarkable woman in many ways – she was not only the first sheriff, but was also the first woman admiral, because in her office of mayor of Southampton, she was also admiral of the port.

The Times obituary pointed out that her special expertise was in the administration of health establishments in the city: 'Under her presidency a progressive policy was followed, and the maternity unit at the municipal hospital and the town's fine system of school clinics are memorials to her period of office. For two years she was President of the Port Sanitary Association.' She died in 1940, aged seventy-six.

We might ask, what is the relationship between the High Sheriff and the Lord Lieutenant? In 1904, a royal warrant was issued, which states that the Lord Lieutenant will have pre-eminence before the High Sheriff on all occasions within the limits of their jurisdiction.

There is no doubt that the office of coroner is very important in the justice system, and the office stretches back to the medieval 'crowner' – the sovereign's regional investigator of deaths. In more recent times, notably since a publication called *Jervis on Coroners* in 1829 and then the Coroners' Acts of 1860 and 1887, this important work, in which a court gathers to decide on actions to take after a death, forms the first step in a court-based criminal process, as it is the coroner who officially states that a death is suspicious, and whether a suicide or murder verdict may be open to further scrutiny. There was no question of a coroner's court dealing with criminal liability after 1977.

The laws relating to coroners and their duties date back a very long way, and between the 1920s and the modern regulations there was continued discussion on how and why their duties should be adapted to the changing patterns of investigation in the criminal justice system. In 1926, for instance, one legal correspondent wrote a feature in which it was pointed out that county coroners and their work needed scrutiny. The writer suggested that every county coroner should be full-time, and that 'the functions of county coroners should be extended considerably, and might well include fire inquests and enquiries into the causes of non-fatal road vehicle accidents.... The machinery is provided, and the work would, therefore, be economically done.'

The coroner before 1977 would have had to be the centre of what Sylvia Barnard described as 'a medico-legal investigation with at least the prospect of increased detection of homicide' – and the first woman coroner, Lilian Hollowell, appointed in Norfolk in 1958, would have experienced that responsibility.

Lilian went into her work not long after a shake-up in the coroners' service: in 1936 the Wright Commission found that the country had a composition for coroner's court that included a large number of very small districts. Consequently, there was a reorganization. At the time there were more than 300 coroners' posts, and the commission decided that a proportion of the coroners were not having enough experience of the work. When Lilian Hollowell stepped into the role it was at a time when the number of coroners was being reduced, as a process of rationalization continued after the Wright Commission reported.

Conclusions

A chapter headed 'conclusions' usually invites the reader to share the writer's drawing together of the strands in the narrative. Some of these strands appear to be self-evident: the male-centred world of law; the fight for female education; the individuals who came through and spoke, wrote and suffered, for ideals; and, of course, the legislators who actually worked on legal changes – in many ways, legal revolutions. Yet there are other bundles of stories: the textless histories of those who helped to create the story of women police officers, for example, yet whose achievements are marked only by mentions of their names in archival documents and in private letters. I have to insist, with these people in mind, that where I have singled out particular names for representative tales, I mean the experience to be one of many. Though, naturally, there are some outstanding heroines.

The great French philosopher of prison, Michel Foucault, wrote of the great penitentiary jailhouse, that 'when it is a question of altering the system of imprisonment, opposition does not come from the judicial institutions alone; resistance is to be found not in the prison as penal sanction, but in the prison with all its determinations.' He singled out the nature of a prison as a means of punishment as 'a great edifice that was as hard to change as a massive destructive machine, set in motion'. Foucault's words helped me to understand why, of all the branches of the criminal justice system, prison establishment has been the slowest to absorb women staff fully, as people with a very valuable contribution to make to prisoner care and control. That slowness to change and accept was a revelation to me as I researched this subject.

However, every social history involves a series of revelations to the historian, and this survey has been no exception. What has emerged from this enquiry has been more than a sequence of biographies, with changes in the law as a backdrop. It has also been far more than a story of campaigns for justice. The scope has been deeper and wider. Perhaps Beatrice Webb's explanation of why she wanted to be a social investigator explains better than my own words what the opening of the professions did for women, writing this in her diary:

> I would like to go amongst men and women with a determination to know them; to humbly observe and consider their characteristics; always remembering how much there is in the most inferior individual which is outside and beyond one's understanding.

This expression of a very generalized aim has within it a simple statement concerning the immense latent talent, energy and selflessness within women, and the sad reflection it forces upon the modern reader is that so many countless numbers of women before the Victorian age never had any chance of entering a profession and experiencing the wider world.

This account has entailed a steady gathering of material, which, when assembled, presents some surprising social history, not the least importance of which is surely the very nature of professional status in Britain. It would be hard to deny that such a status is worth fighting for, but it has to be said that when these major professions were in existence, long before women claimed a place in their ranks, a fight was not necessary. All the more impressive, then, is the present situation when work within the criminal justice system is far more complex and varied than in, say, 1800.

One of the most staggering aspects of the stories told here is the extent to which women were involved in social work of all kinds well before they were in the legal professions; they administrated and managed in a variety of places and contexts that today are barely acknowledged, largely because where and why they worked are matters that have fallen into the obscurity of historical scholarship. One example, from an area of life that was vastly important until the early twentieth-century, is the female presence in the workhouses and asylums. On the surface, such things are at best peripheral to an enquiry concerned with the criminal justice system, but on closer inspection, the two areas of activity are very closely related, as a case from Grimsby makes clear.

In November 1919, a group of outstanding and influential people wrote a joint letter to *The Times* on the subject of the 'feeble-minded' in society. Those who signed included the Chief Rabbi and also Cardinal Bourne, and politicians of note including George Lansbury and Henry Hobhouse. They wrote about the limitations of the new Mental Deficiency Act, which had come into force in 1913, and their main concerns were about what was going to happen to those people with severe mental illness in the workhouses:

> We wish to emphasise the moral aspect of the question. There is every indication that this branch of the subject needs careful study.... The evidence so far is conclusive that a feeble-minded person is more easily swayed by vicious influences than a normal person and that mentally defective boys or girls when thrown into bad company are easy prey to immoral and criminal tendencies.

The dignitaries had good cause to worry about such things. Just four months before their letter was published, Mrs Mary Robinson, a Poor Law guardian of Cleethorpes, was killed by Joseph Woodhall. He was found to be insane at court in Lincoln, and therefore sentenced to be detained 'during His Majesty's pleasure'. She was a good woman, robbed of her life while caring for the needy.

Workhouses were intended, as the 'mission statement' of a Norfolk institution proclaimed, 'for the instruction of youth, the encouragement of industry, the relief of want, the support of old age and the comfort of infirmity and pain'. But they also had to cater for the mentally disturbed, from schizophrenics to bipolar depressives.

There had been concern about female staff in workhouses ever since women began to be allowed to work in such places in the 1880s. In fact, just before the new Act was passed there had been a statement made in 1912 by the Chairman of the National Association of the Feeble-Minded, William Chance, to the effect that there were around 20 per cent feeble-minded people in the workhouses and that these conditions were likely to be a particular problem for female guardians who might be faced with 'a need to physically restrain certain inmates when under duress'. How right he was. Chance had pointed out that the workhouses had large numbers of people who could be classified as 'thieves, prostitutes, paupers, inebriates, lunatics and feeble-minded'.

Chance desperately wanted to see 'better protection and control' of people with mental problems in confinement. He was onto something very important, and it was a subject not fully tackled in the new legislation.

There had been terrible problems in the workhouses for many decades, and since the sensational affair of the cruelty at Andover workhouse in 1846, the government had tried to improve conditions for inmates. In a society experiencing the accelerated social change of the Industrial Revolution, there were large numbers of casualties as people could not cope after losing jobs and indeed families. By 1870, one third of the population of England was living in a workhouse of some kind.

In Grimsby, there had been an early workhouse, called a 'House of Industry', since 1834 when the New Poor Law came into practice; then Grimsby was included in the area covered by the Caistor Poor Law Union. By the end of the century, however, the new workhouse in Scartho Road had been built, opened in 1894 by the Right Honourable J. Shaw-Lefevre. There were separate blocks for the various types of inmate, as the Ordnance Survey map for 1906 shows. So-called 'imbeciles' were housed on the eastern side of the site. But of course terms such as 'imbeciles' and 'feeble-minded' were blanket terms for all kinds of mental illness, from eccentricity to sheer psychopathic natures. For instance, the 'Laceby Hermit', Bobby Marples, spent time in the workhouse after his hut on the Laceby to Aylesby Road was burnt down. Of course, Bobby's case is merely one extreme example; he was not a homicidal maniac. Unfortunately, Mary Robinson did meet one such type that fateful day in July 1919.

A man who would have been included in that group often called the 'despair and reproach of the criminal law' was in Scartho Road when Mrs Robinson was going about her work. With hindsight, it is hard to believe how vulnerable workhouse staff were in these situations: under the various Lunacy Acts, even after the long debate on the 'feeble-minded' staff at Scartho Road still operated for a long time on a system whereby staff were locked in with lunatic inmates until a decision was reached as to whether they merited a transfer to the massive asylum at Bracebridge, south of Lincoln, or not. The supposed lunatics would be in the workhouse on a fourteen-day order until the decision was made.

Basically, the vulnerability of those good people staffing the workhouses went on for some considerable time. Mrs Robinson was one of the unluckiest ones.

While researching and writing this book, I was aware that I was charting a truly significant thread in the great, rich fabric of British history. Such hugely significant events and achievements kept arriving and claiming a place in the story. Yet there are still galling and irritating features of the staffing of our criminal law that – even in 2014 – one is still astonished that more progress has not been made.

For instance, as I write this in October 2014, one newspaper has reported that 'less than a quarter of British judges are women'. The same article points out that in Hungary, 69 per cent of the judiciary is female; in Romania the figure is 72 per cent. Yet when we look closer to home, we find that in Scotland, 78 per cent of that body is male, and in England and Wales the figure is 74.8 per cent male. The writer of that feature in the *i* newspaper, Paul Gallagher, notes, 'Earlier this year, Britain's only female Supreme Court judge called for more gender equality across the legal system – which she believes would improve the quality of justice. Baroness Hale said, "There has only ever been one female Head of Division and in the Supreme Court there is only me. It speaks volumes."'

It would be an understandable response to lament that the long history I have outlined here does not culminate in a total triumph, and that in fact, all the struggles have led only to a partial victory. In one sense, that might be a valid argument, but in the sense of validating what we see around us – the female presence in the law as seen on the streets and in offices – there is evidence enough that there is cause for celebration and congratulation.

In 1895, a book was published with the title *The Builders of our Law*, by Edward Manson. It comprised short biographies of thirty judges in Victoria's reign. In 1938, William Holdsworth wrote *Some Makers of English Law*, featuring accounts of more than twenty judges – all men. Judges do, and always have, made law, by their decisions in court of course, but surely we would like to think that before long, a similar volume will appear and there will be stories of women lawmakers, sitting for the camera, proudly wearing those distinctive wigs. (See plate 23)

Perhaps, if we try to pinpoint a moment at which a certain qualification has to be placed on the success that came with the vote for all adult women in 1928, it is, as Annette Mayer wrote in her survey of the period, that political initiatives were not taken and maximized. Mayer wrote: 'What disappointed feminists was the fact that, despite having an opportunity to press for equal opportunities, women allowed their political attitudes to be shaped by male-directed trends in national politics.' But one response to that has to be that there would not have been sufficient women-centred power in Westminster at the most important time.

One pattern that comes through in the two centuries of social history I have traced here is the immensity of the obstacles to women in their aims to forge a life outside the home – something just as massive within the family as outside, in legislation and in entrenched attitudes. Inside the family, there has always been a tendency to allot roles – and consequently destinies – and in ages past, with so many large middle-class families with plenty of daughters, so many aims and aspirations must have been quashed by the constrictions of one's expected and defined trajectory of life. There is a whole, detailed but scattered, history of the unfulfilled aspirations of Britain's middle-class daughters waiting to be gathered and ordered, but for now, suffice it to say that the ones who did grab themselves an education usually had remarkable achievement on their CVs.

In short, so many of the women's lives featured in my stories illustrate how women have had to succeed in overcoming the obstacles made by dominant ideologies, and then face a second block on their road to success – prejudice. Once again, as in so much historical material, the thinking behind this lies in pictures from popular culture so much more strongly than in literary and worthy productions. This is in a postcard, showing a suffragette tied to some railings, and a policeman walks by, saying, 'Tethered and waiting for your oats, Miss?' (See plate 24)

The great metanarrative of the striving for personal fulfilment and for public service was all around the artist who produced that image, and he chose a cheap laugh, but he did not have the last one.

Yet, in spite of this strain of satire running through the story, it may be said with confidence that the female presence in the justice system has always been there: the fact that it was invisible for a very long time is something to be lamented, but also to be recognized and celebrated, because the contribution of women to all aspects of court, prison and police work has been immense, and the signs are that it will continue to grow and be even more of a force for good.

Acknowledgements

Thanks go to my editor, Linne Matthews, who encouraged this project from the beginning and helped all the way.

Other people have helped with the development of this book as well. In particular, I would like to thank writer and ex-police officer Joan Lock, who provided some of the pictures and whose memoir, *Lady Policeman*, proved to be an invaluable source. Ruth Saunders kindly supplied the pictures relating to her grandmother, Mary Anne Bullock. At the Lincolnshire Archives, Rob Waddington and Mike Rogers were very helpful in accessing photographic material for my illustrations.

Sue Dalton, at Ripon Museum Trust, very kindly let me use the images of the Northallerton prison staff and the Collators' notice (which was originally used in Halifax). I was particularly grateful for the prison picture, as any images of female prison staff before 1900 are hard to find. I have also drawn on my own previous work on prison history, principally on my *House of Care*, a history of Northallerton Prison (now closed).

For images taken from the archives of the Metropolitan Women Police Association, thanks go to Kathy Schuller, who helped in the search for a range of pictures covering most of the period detailed here. There were related oral history sources used here too, and thanks go to Sandra Wilkinson, who kindly allowed me to interview her on her work as a police officer and as a clerical worker during the investigation of the Moors Murders.

At the Old Nick Theatre in Gainsborough, which is a former police station, the curator, Eleanor Bowker, was a great help, clearing the women police officers' room for my photo to be taken.

It would have been very difficult to find first-hand accounts of police officers in the inter-war years without the oral history sources used and reproduced by the writer Norman Lucas, and his book, along with Paul Williams's *Murder Files* roll of honour CD, opened up some very relevant stories.

Finally, Bryan Longbone, an invaluable source for material related to railway history, has to be thanked for enlightening conversations on that topic.

Bibliography and Sources

In a history that aims to cover so much diversity in the sources, there are bound to be gaps, but I have tried to compensate for a shortage of sources in some areas by relying on memoirs as much as on any official documents. A case in point is the baffling lack of material relating to women prison officers' lives between c1910 and 1950. Fortunately, one or two large surveys included some first-hand testimony from individuals. Family history sources proved to be invaluable in this.

As is usually the case in an enquiry into social history in which there has been a certain factor of 'invisibility' as far as the records go, there has been a reliance on such materials as brief newspaper obituaries in some cases, rather than full biographical details. That has been similar to assembling a jigsaw when it came to some provincial and local dignitaries, but I have, understandably, left out some of the smaller cuttings and paragraphs in these cases.

I have relied on many of the byways of history here – necessarily, I feel. The reason is that it is in memoirs that the actual feel of work is conveyed. In the Victorian period, writers and publishers worked to provide documentary fictional accounts of women detectives, for instance, and in comparison with the twentieth-century accounts of a similar kind, the authentic feel of the real experience comes through; but still, I have made use of both.

Books

Note: dates of first publication are shown in brackets before the main details.

Contemporary/Primary Sources

Anon, *Report of the General Committee of the National Union of Women Workers*, NUWW, London, 1895.

Adams, W.H. Davenport, *A Book of Earnest Lives*, Sonnenschein, London, 1884.

French, Yvonne (ed), *News from the Past 1895-1887: The Autobiography of the Nineteenth Century*, Gollancz, London, 1910.

Grove, Trevor, *The Juryman's Tale*, Bloomsbury, London, 1998.

Gurney, Joseph, *Notes Made on a Visit to some of the Prisons of Scotland*, Archibald Constable, London, 1819.

Hamilton, Susan, (ed), *Criminals, Idiots, Women and Minors*, Broadview Press, Peterborough, Ontario, 2004.

Hobhouse, Stephen and Brockway, Fenner, *English Prisons Today*, Longmans, Green & Co, London, 1922.
Holmes, Thomas, *Known to the Police*, Edward Arnold, London, 1908.
Howard, John, *The State of the Prisons* (1777), Dent, London, 1929.
Lytton, Constance, *Prisons and Prisoners* (1914), Virago, London, 1988.
Mass Observation sources: from Sheridan, Dorothy, *Wartime Women*, Phoenix, London, 1990.
Mayhew, Henry, and Binny, John, *The Criminal Prisons of London*, Griffin, Bohn & Co, London, 1862.
Mr Punch in Wig and Gown: the lighter side of bench and bar, The Educational Book Co, London, no date stated.
Nield, Basil, *Farewell to the Assizes*, Garnstone Press, London, 1972.
Pettifer, Ernest W., *The Court is Sitting*, Bradford: Clegg and Sons, no date, but approximately 1960.
Pinkerton, Allan, *Thirty Years a Detective*, Patterson Smith, New Jersey, 1975.
Rolph, C.H., *London Particulars*, OUP, Oxford, 1980.
Sandbach, J B., *This Old Wig*, The Right Book Club, London, 1944.
Sorabji, Cornelia, *India Calling: The Memories of Cornelia Sorabji*, Nisbet, London, 1934.
Sorabji, Cornelia, *The Purdahmashin*, Thacker, Sink & Co, Calcutta, 1917.
St Clair Stobart, Mrs, *War and Women*, G. Bell, London, 1913.
Strahan, J.A., *The Bench and Bar of England*, Blackwood, London, 1919.
The Public General Statutes 1919, Eyre & Spottiswoode, London, 1919.
Tristan, Flora, *The London Journal* (1942), Virago, London, 1982.
Woolf, Virginia, *A Room of One's Own* (1929) and *Three Guineas* (1938), Penguin, London, 1993.
Wootton, Barbara, *In a World I Never Made: autobiographical reflections*, George Allen & Unwin, London, 1967.

Secondary Sources/Works Cited

Amos, Sir Maurice, *British Justice*, The British Council, London, 1940.
Arthur, Max, *Lost Voices of the Edwardians*, Harper Perennial, London, 2007.
Barnard, Sylvia, M., *Viewing the Breathless Corpse*, Quacks the Printers, York, 2001.
Bennett, Daphne, *Emily Davies and the Liberation of Women*, Andre Deutsch, London, 1990.
Bourke, Joanna, *What it Means to be Human*, Virago, London, 2011.
Brown, Douglas (ed), *A Book of Modern Prose*, Harrap, London, 1957.
Cadbury, Geraldine S., *Young Offenders: Yesterday and Today*, George Allen & Unwin, London, 1938.
Cecil, Henry, *The Trial of Walter Rowland*, David & Charles, London, 1978.
Cockcroft, Irene, and Croft, Susan, *Art, Theatre and Women's Suffrage*, Aurora Metro, London, 2010.

Conrad, Joseph, *Heart of Darkness* (1902), Wordsworth Editions, Ware, 1999.
Cooke, Rachel, *Her Brilliant Career*, Virago, London, 2013.
Cowley, Richard, *A History of the British Police*, The History Press, Stroud, 2011.
Emsley, Clive, *The Great British Bobby*, Quercus, London, 2009.
Fido, Martin, and Skinner, Keith, *The Official Encyclopaedia of Scotland Yard*, Virgin, London, 1999.
Foucault, Michel, *Discipline and Punish: the birth of the prison*, Penguin, London, 1977.
Gladwin, Irene, *The Sheriff: The Man and his Office*, McCartney, London, 1984.
Goopta, Suparna, *Cornelia Sorabji: India's Pioneer Woman Lawyer*, OUP, Delhi, 2006.
Green, Jonathon, *Crooked Talk: five hundred years of the language of crime*, Random House, London, 2011.
Haining, Peter, *The Golden Age of Crime Fiction*, Prion, London, 2002.
Hall, Jean Graham, and Smith, Gordon D., *R v Bywaters and Thompson*, Barry Rose Publishers, Chichester, 1997.
Harman, Harriet, and Griffith, John, *Justice Deserted: the subversion of the jury*, National Council for Civil Liberties, London, 1979.
Heidensohn, Frances, *Women in Control?*, Clarendon Press, Oxford, 1992.
Hollis, Patricia, *Ladies Elect: women in English local government 1865-1914*, Clarendon Press, Oxford, 1987.
Horn, Pamela, *Flappers*, Amberley, Stroud, 2013.
Jones, Enid Huws, *Margery Fry: The Essential Amateur*, OUP, London, 1986.
Leech, Mark, and Cheney, Deborah, *The Prisons Handbook*, Waterside Press, London, annual.
Liebling, Alison *et alia*, *The Prison Officer*, Willan, Abingdon, 2011.
Livingston, Stephen, and Owen, Tim, *Prison Law*, OUP, Oxford, 1993.
Lucas, Norman, *WPC 'Courage'*, Weidenfeld & Nicolson, London, 1986.
Mappen, Ellen, *Helping Women at Work*, Hutchinson, London, 1985.
Mayer, Annette, *Women in Britain 1900-2000*, Hodder & Stoughton, Abingdon, 1998.
Moir, Esther, *The Justice of the Peace*, Penguin, London, 1969.
Moss, Alan, and Skinner, Keith, *The Scotland Yard Files: Milestones in Crime Detection*, The National Archives, London, 2006.
Mossman, Mary Jane, *The First Women Lawyers*, OUP, Oxford, 2006.
Nown, Graham, *Watching the Detectives*, Grafton Books, London, 1991.
Page, Martin, *Crime Fighters of London*, Inner London Probation Service, London, 2002.
Priestley, Philip, *Victorian Prison Lives*, Pimlico, London, 1999.
Proctor, Tammy M., *Female Intelligence*, New York University Press, New York, 2003.

Robinson, Jane, *Bluestockings*, Penguin, London, 2009.
Rowbotham, Sheila, *Friends of Alice Wheeldon*, Pluto Press, London, 1986.
Saunders, John B., *Mozley and Whiteley's Law Dictionary*, Butterworths, London, 1977.
Schulz, Dorothy Moses, *Breaking the Brass Ceiling: Women Police Sheriffs and Their Paths to the Top*, Greenwood, Westport, CT, 1985.
Shandler, Nina, *The Strange Case of Hellish Nell*, Da Capo Press, Philadephia, 2006.
Shaw, Bernard, *The Apple Cart* (1929), Penguin, London, 1970.
Shoolbred, C.F., *The Administration of Criminal Justice in England and Wales*, Pergamon Press, Oxford, 1966.
Shpayer-Makov, Haia, *The Ascent of the Detective*, OUP, Oxford 2011.
Skyrme, Sir Thomas, *The Changing Image of the Magistracy*, Macmillan Press, Basingstoke, 1979.
Thomas, J.E., *The English Prison Officer since 1850*, Routledge & Kegan Paul, London, 1972.
Turner, *The Women's Bar Association of Illinois: The First 75 Years*, Women's Bar Association of Illinois, 1991.
Worsfold, T. Cato, *Staple Inn and its Story*, Samuel Bagster, London, 1913.
Wroath, John, *Until They are Seven*, Waterside Press, London, 1998.

Other Reference Sources
British Nineteenth Century Newspapers: Gengage sources
Interview with Rose Mary Braithwaite: The Cohen Interviews, University of Warwick, edited by Tim Cook and Harry Marsh, www2.warwick.ac.uk/services/ibrary/mrc/exploresurther/subject_guides/social_work
The Medico-Criminological Review, (Medico-Legal Society, London, October 1934.
Home Office Report of the Departmental Committee on Detective Work and Procedure Vol.1, HMSO, London, 1938.
The Recruitment of People with Higher Educational Qualification into the Police Service, HMSO, London, 1967.
The Criminal Justice Act 1948, Butterworth, London, 1949.
The Liberal Publication Department: *The Government's Record 1906-1913*, Liberal Publications Department, London, 1913.
Royal Commission on Justices of the Peace 1946-48 Report, HMSO, London, 1948.
The Times Digital Archive
The Times: Obituary of Rose Heilbron, 13 December 2005.

Educational Material
Johnson, David, *London's Peelers and the British Police*, Jackdaw Publications, London, 1970.

Articles/Essays

Anon, 'Child Offenders', *The Times*, 29 August 1917, p.3.
Anon, '"Good Morning Ladies" Called the Prison Governor', *The Times*, 12 February 1964, p.7.
Anon, 'Hilary Heilbron on Writing the Life of her Mother', *Liverpool Echo*, 21 September 2014.
Anon, 'Law in Practice', *The Times*, 10 July 1922, p.4.
Anon, 'The Law Society', *The Times*, 23 June 1932, p.4.
Anon, Local Law Societies in *The Law Society Gazette*, 2 May 1973, p.1,755.
Anon, 'The High Sheriff', *The Times*, 26 April 1925, p.11.
Bew, John, 'Welfare Wrapped in a Patriotic Flag', *New Statesman*, 4 December 2014, pp.35-39.
Crosland, Erthel, 'Nina Blyth', *Probation Journal*, April 1933, p.235.
Gallagher, Paul, 'Less than a Quarter of British Judges are Women', in *i* newspaper, 10 October 2014, p.28.
Hayes, Michelle, 'Promotion and Management: What Choice for Women?', *Probation Journal*, Vol.36 No.1, March 1989, pp.12-17.
Jackson, Louise A., 'Lilian Mary Elizabeth Wyles', *The Dictionary of National Biography* online: www.oxforddnb.com/templates/article.jsp?articeid=97945&back
Kumari, Neelama, Caulfield, Laura, and Newberry, Michelle, 'The Experiences of Women Working in a Male Therapeutic Community Prison', *The Prison Service Journal*, May 2012, No.201, pp.7-11.
Lock, Joan, 'Grantham's other First Lady', *Journal of the Police History Society*, No.21, 2006, pp.5-6.
McCarthy, Helen, 'Opening the Doors of Diplomacy', *History Today*, Vol.64 No.8, August 2014, p.3.
Obituary: Dame Rose Heilbron, *The Times*, 13 December 2005.
Polden, Patrick, 'The Lady of Tower Bridge: Sybil Campbell, England's First Woman Judge', *Women's History Review*, 8:3, 505-526 online.
Rowland, David, biographical sketch of Margaret Damer Dawson, Old Police Cells Museum site, www.oldpolicecellsmusem.org.uk
Workman, Joanne, 'Helena Florence Normanton', Dictionary of National Biography online, www.oxforddnb.com/templates/article.jsp?articleid=39091&back
Wright, Allen W., 'Interviews in Sherwood', www.boldoutlaw.com/ronint/

Archives

British Federation of University Women 1955 records, Lincolnshire Archives.
Matron's Journals 1848-1868, from Lincoln Castle Prison, Lincolnshire Archives.
Women's Voluntary Service New Sheet, No.12, September 1962.
WVS Houses for Ex-Borstal Boys, from my own archive of crime documents.

Online Sources

www.ncjrs.gov/App/publications/abstract.aspx?ID+139694
www.policememorial.org.uk
'Policewomen on the Railways', British Transport Police, see www.btp.police.uk
www.tameside.gov.uk/blueplaque/adasummers, see this site for an account of Ada Summers, the first woman to adjudicate on an English Bench: she was one of the first women to be appointed a JP.
'A Tribute to Ada Summers, MBE, JP'
Murder Files at www.murderfiles.com. This is a database of the unlawful killing of British police officers, produced by Paul Williams, who also compiled the listings on two CDs under the title *The Ultimate Price*.

Periodicals consulted:

Police Review
Prison Service Journal
The Daily Graphic
The Daily Telegraph
The Illustrated Police News

Police Records and Museums

Note: for help with research into women in police history, in addition to the organizations on websites listed above, there are two particular sources that provide a large, general police history repository of materials:

The Police History Society: www.policehistorysociety.co.uk
The Open University database: www.open.ac.uk/Arts/history/policing/police-archives-guide

These are the foremost museums for police history. For a complete listing, see the annual publication, *The Family and Local History Handbook* (Blatchford Publishing, York).

British Transport Police History Society, 15-17 Tavistock Place, London WC1 9SY.
Garda Siochana Museum and Archives, The Records Tower, Dublin Castle, Dublin 2.
The Glasgow Police Museum, 68 St Andrew's Square, Glasgow G1 5PR.
The Hampshire Constabulary History Society, Southern Support and Training Headquarters, Victoria House, Netley, Hampshire.
Imperial War Museums, Lambeth Road, London SE1 6HZ.
The Metropolital Police, MPS Records Management Branch, Empress State Building, Lille Road, London SW6 1TR.

National Police Library, Centrex, Bramshill, Hook, Hampshire RG27 0JW.
North Eastern Police History Society, Brinkburn Cottage, 28 Brinkburn High Street, Barnes, Sunderland SR4 7RG.
The Police History Society, Secretary, 64 Nore Marsh Road, Wootton Bassett, Wiltshire SN4 8BH.
Police Officers' Roll of Honour Trust, PO Box 999, Preston PR4 5WW.
Research into Family and Police History, 52 Symons Avenue, Eastwood, Leigh-on-Sea, Essex SS9 5QE.
Ripon Prison and Police Museum, St Marygate, Ripon, North Yorkshire HG4 1LX.
Surrey Police Museum, Mount Browne, Sandy Lane, Guildford, Surrey GU3 1HG.
Thames Valley Police Museum, Sulhamstead, Nr Reading, Berkshire RG7 4DX.
West Midlands Police Museum, Sparkhill Police Station, Stratford Road, Sparkhill, Birmingham, West Midlands B11 4EA.

Index